Deaf Side Story

Deaf Side Story

Deaf Sharks, Hearing Jets, and a Classic American Musical

Mark Rigney

Gallaudet University Press
Washington, D.C.

Gallaudet University Press
Washington, D.C. 20002
http://gupress.gallaudet.edu

Note: Though every effort was made to secure the permission of each individual described in this work, some names have been changed to protect the identities of those individuals who could not be contacted.

Library of Congress Cataloging-in-Publication Data

Rigney, Mark.
   Deaf side story : deaf Sharks, hearing Jets, and a classic American musical / Mark Rigney.
      p. cm.
   Includes bibliographical references and index.
   ISBN 1-56368-145-5
   1. Musicals—United States—History and criticism. 2. Musicals—United States—Production and direction. 3. Deaf musicians. 4. Bernstein, Leonard, 1918—West Side story. I. Title.

ML2054.R54 2003
792.6'42—dc22   2003049301

∞ The paper used in this publication meets the minimum requirements of American National Standard for Information Sciences—Permanence of Paper for Printed Library Materials, ANSI Z39.48-1984.

For Philip H. Decker
. . . because of what he said

Contents

Author's Note

When chronicling a project designed to break down cultural barriers, it seems to me foolish to erect new ones, and so, in keeping with the general informality of the theatrical process, I have chosen to refer to the people who grace these pages by their first names. In a similar vein, because theater naturally and eternally exists in the present, I have intentionally recorded the events that follow in present tense. If I have a regret, it is only that I do not know any form of sign language. Still, I like to think that I have made every effort to deliver as balanced a portrait of both Deaf culture and the project as a whole as any hearing person may reasonably be expected to achieve. Errors in chronology, and they are few, I chalk up to artistic license. Minor errors in the messy business of quotation I have come to accept as necessities, especially when dealing with words initially delivered in a foreign language (such as American Sign Language or, depending, English). For errors in fact, however, I have no patience. Should any exist within these pages, the fault lies entirely with me, and not in any way with the many wonderful and generous people who have assisted with this manuscript.

Acknowledgments

For their time and insights, my thanks to the many cast, crew, and creative team members who assisted in this project. For their support and cooperation, both tacit and explicit, I would like to thank the administration of MacMurray College, especially President Lawrence Bryan and Dean Jim Goulding, as well as Superintendent Joan Forney and High School Principal Steve Tavender at the Illinois School for the Deaf. Finally, to my dedicated editors at Gallaudet University Press, Ivey Pittle Wallace and Deirdre Mullervy, my deep gratitude for their help in shaping and directing this book.

Overture

On Sunday, February 6, in the year 2000, one full day before the start of rehearsals for *West Side Story*, director Diane Brewer discovers through a newspaper photograph that her leading man, the actor slated to play Tony, has effectively dropped out of the show. It is something of a fluke that she sees the photo at all. It's midsize, black-and-white, and it hides on the inside page of Jacksonville's skinny, long-suffering paper, the *Journal-Courier*. Scanning quickly from article to article, Diane gives the photo only the briefest glance, but then the face in the picture registers and she looks more closely. The photograph shows Scott Corbin, a sophomore at Illinois College (IC), busily auditioning, not for *West Side Story*, Diane's production, but for *Godspell*, to be presented concurrently at the local community theater. The first words out of her mouth are, "This must be a misprint. That can't be Scott." She peers closer, remembering a rumor that Scott has a twin brother. "That," she says, "doesn't even look like Scott."

Her disbelief is understandable. Scott Corbin has already spent several sessions with *West Side Story*'s music director, pianist, and vocal coach Terri Benz. Although he's been difficult to schedule and tends to have mysterious car trouble, Scott has sung well enough to keep Terri enthusiastic. On February 3, just days before his Saturday audition for *Godspell*, Scott had told Terri how excited he was about landing the role of Tony, about how he couldn't wait for rehearsals to start. He said he loved singing, loved musicals. Terri wondered if his excessive enthusiasm was really on the level, but after only four vocal rehearsals, she decided she didn't know her pupil well enough to judge. In any event, as far as either Terri or Diane could see, Scott understood full well that Tony is one of the truly plum roles in all of musical theater and he intended to make the most of his opportunity.

In retrospect, one of Scott's troubles may have been the ease with which he landed the part. He would have had no shot at all had any viable tenors tried out from MacMurray College (Mac), the school actually putting on the production. Scott, essentially a rival from down the street, came into the picture only when it became depressingly evident that the few able singers at Mac had no intention of auditioning. Diane placed a call to the choir director at IC, asking for leads and recommendations. Scott's name came up, and when he demonstrated that he could—almost—sing the part, the role was suddenly his.

Diane responds to the photograph by calling Phil Funken-bush, *Godspell*'s director and the resident theater columnist for the *Illinois Times*, the Springfield-based equivalent of the *Phoenix* or the *Village Voice*. Phil isn't overly surprised to hear from Diane because Scott, like all those auditioning for *Godspell*, had to fill out a sheet listing potential conflicts and other commitments. He wrote down "No conflicts." One of Phil's assistants thought that sounded fishy and asked Scott if he wasn't already in *West Side Story*. Scott replied that yes, he was, but he really wanted to do *Godspell* instead. Phil thanked him for coming and made a mental note not to cast him. Later, Phil and his team joked about how ironic it would be if the *Journal-Courier* printed, as its one picture of the audition process, the shot they'd taken of Scott. Wouldn't he be surprised? they said, not ever expecting it to occur.

As of Sunday afternoon, none of the *Godspell* cast has been notified as to their status one way or the other. Diane thanks Phil for the information and hangs up. She taps the phone against her palm and stares out the window. "I can't believe he's doing this," she says aloud, referring to Scott. "He has the opportunity to play Tony! Doesn't he understand?"

Scott makes the defection official the next day, not with a telephone call or a meeting in person, but with an e-mail (which Diane has not, to this day, graced with a reply):

> This e-mail is in response to a scheduling conflict. I've wanted to do *Godspell* since I was fifteen. . . . Then I got Tony, and took it, since I hadn't planned on making it. Well, I was told by someone who made the [*Godspell*] cast that I had made it. . . . I thought long and hard, straining my brain to think which one was right for me. I realized that my heart was telling me that *Godspell* was the one. I will do whatever it takes to help you, in case you want suggestions in finding a replacement. (2/7/00)

As it turns out, Phil Funkenbush is just as perturbed as Diane by Scott's duplicity and, contrary to the rumors Scott had heard, declines to cast him. Thus Scott's decision to audition for *Godspell* effectively puts him, at least for the spring of 2000, on a Jacksonville-wide theatrical blacklist.

Scott's departure becomes the third domino in a steadily increasing chain. The first to withdraw was a Mac student who had signed on to play Doc; the second, a high school student suspended for smoking pot. He would have been one of the Jets. By the end of the first rehearsal, Diane has lost three Jets. It is an inauspicious beginning that only gets worse. By the end of the rehearsal process, no fewer than nine performers will have dropped out of the show.

Thirty more make it through, and half of that number are deaf.

Prologue

[Jacksonville] is a horribly ugly village, composed of little shops and dwellings which stuck close together around a dingy square, in the middle of which stands the ugliest of possible brick courthouses, with a spire and a weathercock on its top.

William Cullen Bryant, 1832

Jacksonville, Illinois, sits on the fold of the map some thirty-five miles west of Springfield, the state capital. Interstate 72 races past, intent on reaching the Iowa border. Corn and soybeans dominate the landscape; the last vestiges of native prairie have long since been plowed under. Clusters of farm buildings hide among stands of aged oak and maple; silvery bullet-shaped silos tower on their flanks. The largest north-south route through town is Highway 67, connecting Alton, Greenfield, and Jacksonville with Beardstown and Macomb to the north. The town and the state have plans to expand the road into a four-lane limited-access expressway. The going, so far, has been slow. West of town, a new bridge has been built, but the entry ramps lead nowhere except back, like a chute, into the fields.

The town is old, founded in 1825. A surveyor by the name of Johnston Shelton laid out the plat, beginning with 160 acres centered on a 5-acre public square. The lone inhabitant within that incipient town boundary was Alexander Cox, a hatter whom history has otherwise forgotten. One early settler, Mrs. John Tilson, wrote home to her East Coast mother: "I can stand in the middle of my one-room log cabin, take a cat by the tail, and sling it in any direction between the logs, out of doors."

Jacksonville's subsequent history comes laden with tales of temperance unions and the long, angry shadows of the Civil War. Governor Joseph Duncan lived here in the 1830s when Jacksonville briefly served as the state capital, and his house, the Duncan Mansion, is now a national historic shrine, owned and maintained by the local chapter of the Daughters of the American Revolution. More than a few of the grander homes on State Street are reminiscent of the Old South, vaguely antebellum and definitely wealthy. Around the edges of the town, however, the poorer side of the Midwest holds sway: Jacksonville has several trailer parks and each one seems full to the brim. Not that buying a house is an outrageously expensive proposition. In 1996, the last year that the chamber of commerce gathered such statistics, the average purchase price for a home was only $85,000.

William E. Sullivan invented the Big Eli Wheel in Jacksonville, the world's first portable Ferris wheel. He founded the Eli Bridge Company, which continues to fill occasional orders for more. Fans of Drew Barrymore can watch her ride a Big Eli Wheel in the movie *Never Been Kissed*. For those who prefer to experience their amusement rides firsthand, Big Eli no. 17, well lit and beautifully maintained, stands in the large, wooded Community Park at the intersection of Main Street and Morton Avenue. On certain summer evenings, the wheel is open to the public and you can ride it, up and around, up and around, never quite topping the trees. You do, however, get a fine view of the passing cars because, for now, Main Street and Highway 67 are one and the same. When the bypass is complete, at least some of the traffic on Main Street will disappear.

Morton Avenue is another story entirely. The street is a mecca for shopping and eating. Every inch is lined with chain restaurants, mostly fast food: Long John Silver's, McDonald's, Taco Bell, Wendy's. None of the stores pushing against Morton's curbs cater to the wealthy. Jacksonville has a JC Penney, four competing grocery stores, a Kmart, several car dealerships and of course, a Wal-Mart. The Wal-Mart lot is always twice as crowded as Kmart's. Corporate executives declared the local Hardee's to be the busiest in the franchise. It did so well that the company recently built an entire new building, just ten feet from the old one. When the new restaurant opened, the old facility was summarily demolished.

When Jacksonville residents want to eat out, they have few options besides fast food, pizza, a diner or two, and the buffet at Ponderosa. The classy option is Lonzerotti's, a popular Italian restaurant that occupies the old railway station. The tracks remain active and enormous freight trains rumble past at irregular intervals. The louder ones drown conversation and ripple the merlot in the wine glasses. El Rancherito, a growing Midwest chain, provides the other ethnic alternative, and their menu features all manner of muddy-looking Mexican and Tex-Mex fare. The prices are good, the margaritas both large and weak; the atmosphere, however, pales before the sometimes quiet, sometimes train-ridden ambience of Lonzerotti's. If an after-dinner movie appeals, tickets cost five dollars.

Industry provides jobs for those who do not farm. Wareco, a chain of gasoline stations and convenience shops, is based here. Tenneco (now Pactiv) makes plastic bags, notably Hefty OneZip bags. EMI presses compact discs on the northwest side of town. They remain infamous for asking employees to use clear plastic sacks rather than purses or bags prior to releasing the Beatles compact disc sets in 1995 and 1996. Not far away, Nestlé does a good business making Coffeemate. As alternative industries, Jacksonville boasts an area hospital, Passavant, and a prison. Some local realtors blame the prison for swelling the numbers of run-down homes and cheap trailers. Others claim that the prison has brought a bad element into the area, but nobody seems comfortable defining or identifying what or who exactly this element might be. Jacksonville, despite its official status as a city (population 20,284), remains essentially a small town, and nobody wants to risk insulting someone who may have a relative—or themselves spent time—behind the prison's walls.

Then there are the colleges. MacMurray College and Illinois College are both small, private, liberal arts institutions; their coexistence in such a small community has prompted a popular rumor, possibly true, that Jacksonville boasts more Ph.D.s per capita than any other locale in North America. IC once enrolled only men, whereas Mac began its life as a women's college. Both are now co-ed, or to use the original term, coordinate. Each would like to have about eight hundred students, but Mac, the poor sister, is chronically underenrolled. During the late seventies and early eighties, Mac nearly went bankrupt thanks to half a century of deficit spending. A cycle of heavy borrowing resulted, both from banks and from the school's own endowment.

Meanwhile, IC became among the best-endowed small schools in the country, and its alumni revenues have helped construct a new library, a proscenium theater space, an arts center, and in March 2003, a new athletic facility. IC is thought to be the more conservative of the two institutions, something former graduate and trustee William Jennings Bryan would likely be proud of, but neither institution has a particularly liberal student body as colleges go. Both schools draw heavily from the surrounding community and both rely on church affiliation, Mac with the Methodists and IC with the Congregationalists. At times, and despite their differences, it is difficult to see why the two schools have not simply merged. Indeed, in the 1950s, when Mac was flush and IC was not, Mac's board did float such a proposal. The idea was to make IC the men's campus and keep Mac as the women's campus. Curricula, staff, and administration would have been combined. The schools' presidents held tentative meetings, but when IC's board and alumni heard what was going on, they were, so the story goes, positively apoplectic. The merger quickly fell through.

Despite its recent monetary woes, Mac has proved a difficult beast to kill. It has struggled valiantly back from its former insolvency, and in 1997, Mac's trustees hired a new president, Lawrence Bryan, former head of Kalamazoo College in Michigan. Larry Bryan—unrelated, so far as he knows, to William Jennings Bryan—brought with him a sense of direction and optimism that has, by all accounts, been lacking amongst the school's faculty and staff. Mac, for the first time in decades, appears to be going places.

Concurrent with Bryan's arrival, Mac decided to revitalize a number of moribund programs, including drama. They hired Diane Brewer, a recent Ph.D. graduate of UCLA, and charged her with directing two productions a year, teaching all theater classes, and resurrecting the drama major. Diane is a small woman with small features, and during her first six months on the job, people frequently mistook her for a student. She has straight, brown hair that falls in a line to her shoulders; she prefers informal clothes and eschews makeup. She has no fear of telling offbeat stories in public or supporting these with elaborate facial expressions. If she can't talk with her hands, she often stops talking.

The overall impression is hardly academic, but Mac nonetheless entrusted her with both the job and a nearly abandoned dance studio for a performance space. In her first two years, she produced and directed Glowacki's *Antigone in New York*, Brecht's *A Good Person of Setzuan*, and Moliere's *Tartuffe*. She also brought in Stephen Buescher of California's Dell'Arte Players Company as artist-in-residence for the month of January 1999. Stephen, an ebullient, tremendously talented performer, turned out to have strong ties to the Deaf theater community (the capital D implying a cultural and political sensibility whereby the deaf person in question identifies himself or herself primarily with a community of other deaf or hard-of-hearing people). In 1995, Stephen answered an ad in the magazine *ArtSEARCH* placed by Sunshine Too, the touring theater troupe from the National Technical Institute for the Deaf (NTID) in Rochester, New York. As a guest artist, Stephen joined the company (typically three deaf and three hearing actors) and stayed for three years, eventually taking on writing and directing duties in addition to acting. Stephen, who is hearing, remembers most performances as being "very much in the variety show range," and he worked hard to incorporate the physical techniques of clowning and commedia dell'arte with the equally physical work of sign language—a natural match. In *Laundry*, the vignette Stephen remembers best, he and the other actors portrayed the various stages of washing clothes, running through "rinse," "wash," "sort," and so on. Other segments revolved around racism and Gallaudet's Deaf President Now movement (see chapter seven).

Late in Stephen's MacMurray stay, Diane has an idea—what she describes as little more than a spark, a flash—for the show she will do in the spring of 2000 (still a year away): *West Side Story*.

A musical, especially a performance like the one she envisions, will require a far greater commitment of time, resources, and logistics than any show she has attempted before. From the very beginning, Diane's goal is not merely to put on *West Side Story*, the musical, but to build the show as a joint production between Mac and the Illinois School for the Deaf (ISD). The ISD campus sits on the far side of town, sprawling across fifty acres of residence halls, classrooms, and playing fields. It is the nation's tenth oldest school for deaf students, founded in 1846. Enrollment hovers around the three hundred mark and includes both residential and day students. It boasts an accredited curriculum for kindergarten through twelfth grade, with an emphasis in later grades on vocational, technical, and college preparatory classes. ISD's presence has given rise to a sizable Deaf community in Jacksonville, and for the most part, the town's hearing populace does not bat an eye when encountering a person whose level of hearing does not measure up to their own. Not surprisingly, ISD's proximity to Mac is a major reason why the latter school has had such success (and motivation) in developing its prominent Deaf Education programs.

For Diane, the notion of bringing the two schools together has been brewing for some time, born of watching her Mac actors use sign language to communicate backstage during past shows. Her immediate reaction is that the signing "should be onstage, not behind the scenes." Intrigued, she contacts Rod Lathim, a Southern California director whose mixed company of deaf and hearing actors she'd seen last as a grade-schooler. She asks him what pitfalls to avoid should she embark on a project with deaf and hearing performers, and he tells her to be certain, above all else, to make the work collaborative. If, says Lathim, all you as a hearing person do is direct, you won't achieve anything.

Closer to home, Diane has several reasons for thinking that stage work featuring deaf actors might be a success. First, Mac's Deaf Education majors include many of the school's finest students, most of whom have never shown much interest in theater, but Diane hopes that running a show in conjunction with ISD might give her sudden access to this heretofore untapped pool of talent. Second, strong ties already exist between Mac and ISD, which allows many of Mac's Deaf Ed majors into its classrooms as they prepare to take on classes of their own after graduation. Third, Stephen Buescher's commedia performance, although far from silent (he relies heavily on prerecorded swing music), is wordless. He does not speak, nor is he spoken to, yet he communicates brilliantly with the audience members, many of whom are deaf high schoolers from ISD, invited specially by Diane to attend Buescher's shows. Their enthusiasm, combined with Diane's own, cements her decision to work cast members of differing levels of hearing into an upcoming production.

The pressure for Diane to mount a full-scale musical has been escalating since her arrival, both among Mac's students and also its alumni. The feeling is that only a musical will establish once and for all that Mac theater is back to stay. Unfortunately, Diane herself has little respect for the majority of well-known American musicals and has no desire to involve herself with *Oklahoma!, Pajama Game,* or their ilk. *West Side Story,* however, with its gritty story line of young, thwarted love, seems to her to offer a dose of artistic integrity. The fact that its music will have to be at least partially delivered by deaf or hard of hearing cast members only fuels her interest.

Did Diane have any concrete reason for believing such a production could be successfully staged? Her answer, given in retrospect, is an unadorned "No."

February 11, 1999

At 2:25 P.M., the National Weather Service issues a tornado warning for Morgan County and Jacksonville in particular. A tornado has been identified fifteen miles southwest of the city, heading northwest at fifty miles an hour. Sirens begin going off as roiling clouds and fierce, gusting winds produce driving rain. Actual waves rise up on the larger puddles. Mac students in Rutledge Hall retreat to the basement under the supervision of their building resident assistants and they cower there, waiting for the alert to end. Many bring schoolwork, but they give up on this when the power abruptly goes out at 2:35. Mac is not the only site affected; most of Jacksonville loses power. The winds continue, tearing down trees, peeling the roof off Kmart, and knocking rural barns from their foundations.

The actual tornado never arrives, and the alert officially ends at 3:00.

However, with the power out, the tornado sirens cannot sound the all clear. This maroons the Mac students in the dark, increasingly stuffy basement. Across town, ISD suffers a similar fate, with the end result that a planned meeting between Diane, Bob Dramin, Cara Hammond, and Paula Chance (the latter two from ISD) gets postponed indefinitely. This would have been their second official meeting, but only Bob, an instructor at Mac in the Deaf and Hard of Hearing Teacher Education program, makes it to Rutledge Hall, accompanied by an interpreter. Bob is a mild, thickset man with a heavy neck, his close-cropped black hair beginning to gray. In cool weather, he favors a teal Eddie Bauer jacket and blue jeans. Bob and Diane decide that there is no point in waiting for the ISD contingent, because the storm will force them to keep watch over their students. When Bob and Diane converse, Diane looks at Bob throughout, even when waiting for the interpreter to complete the process of signing what she has said. It is considered bad manners in the Deaf community for the hearing conversant to make eye contact or talk directly to the interpreter. (One is not, after all, having the conversation with the interpreter.) Bob, however, looks at Diane when he is signing and then watches the interpreter to see Diane's response.

Diane has opted to audit Bob's American Sign Language (ASL) course in preparation for the upcoming production. The class has been helpful, and today she finds that she recognizes some of the hand and body motions Bob makes, but not enough to comprehend their full meaning. This only serves to underscore the fact that, without the interpreter, the meeting could not take place, storm or no storm. The interpreter, however, has only been contracted to work until four. At four o'clock, she will head for home, and so, even if the ISD contingent were to arrive, the meeting would end abruptly with her departure. Nor is the interpreter likely to stick around out of some sense of altruism or

charity. Within the Deaf community, the dominant school of
thought holds that interpreters should not lend their services free
of charge. Thus, for the interpreter to remain of her own volition
after four o'clock would be an ethical violation. Even if the interpreter wanted to stay—and had no other commitments—she
would, in effect, be honor-bound to leave. Diane or Bob could
offer to pay her for additional time, but given the weather delays
and missing personnel, this seems pointless to everyone involved.

The meeting officially ends at 3:20. Later, using a still-
working home phone, Diane manages to reach Cara Hammond,
a Mac graduate, class of '95, currently employed as a speech
pathologist at ISD. Cara reports that ISD's students are still in
the basement and that Diane and Bob made the right decision.
Cara, who is hearing, tentatively reschedules the meeting for the
next week, but in the end, that meeting too is canceled, due to
scheduling conflicts.

One meeting has already taken place, in late January of
1999 (a full sixteen months before the scheduled production
run). Diane, Bob, and Ruth-Ann Hecker, also with Mac's Deaf
Education Department, attend. This is the first formal meeting
held on *West Side Story*'s behalf, and it serves as a springboard for
ideas and hurdles that will later be dealt with in staging and performance. Diane lays out her basic goal of merging the talents of
the Deaf Ed and Theater Departments with those of ISD, and
Ruth-Ann reacts by flatly stating that *West Side Story* "shouldn't
be a Deaf issues play."

Diane, who has no desire to deviate from the play's basic
text (a violation of copyright law), agrees, but stresses that she
does not want to produce a play featuring deaf performers that
essentially ignores the presence of deaf actors on the stage. Con-
nections, and people failing to connect, are ongoing fascinations
for Diane in her theater work. With *West Side Story*, she wants
recommendations from Ruth-Ann and Bob on how best to deal
with interpreting onstage. Ruth-Ann and Bob describe two basic

and accepted styles of onstage interpreting, Simultaneous Communication (SimCom) and shadow (or shadowing).

An actor using SimCom signs and speaks at the same time. In addition to performing arts settings, SimCom is often used in educational settings, sometimes in conjunction with other manual and visual cues. Within the Deaf theater community, the general feeling is that SimCom, while easy on the eye, becomes in practice an inherent betrayal of the text. Because word-for-word translation between spoken English and ASL is not possible, the resultant signed message becomes an inexpressive shorthand for English, and the underlying meaning is lost. To further complicate matters, speaking and signing simultaneously drastically limits facial expression, which might be like skipping every fifth word in a speech. Finally, because spoken words flow off the tongue faster than the hands can sign, actors must slow down their oral delivery to use SimCom.

Shadowing has its own drawbacks, because it assumes that a given actor cannot sign and therefore must have a double following him or her around the stage. During a recent performance of Willy Conley's *Broken Spokes* at Chicago's Bailiwick Theatre, the interpreters remained seated downstage right throughout the performance, even when the rest of the cast had retreated to the opposite end of the stage, a technique known as stationary interpreting. Diane, who saw *Broken Spokes,* does not want to follow in that show's footsteps. She tells Bob and Ruth-Ann that she wants *West Side Story*'s interpretation to be integrated, to ebb and flow, to move in sync with the onstage action.

Even providing interpreters will be a challenge, because no one expects the interpreters to volunteer their services (except in casual conversation or with friends). Unfortunately, this has the effect of hog-tying *West Side Story,* because the budget of the show cannot absorb the cost of a full-time interpreter through the projected nine weeks of rehearsal. No one has an immediate solution.

Ruth-Ann, meanwhile, mentions another aspect of interpreting, and that is an interpreter's effective neutrality—sometimes tacit, often explicit—in any given situation. She brings up
Stephen Buescher's commedia performance as an example, stressing that Stephen "violated [the interpreter's] code of ethics."
Stephen, playing a poverty-stricken clown named Arlecchino,
chose to interact directly with the interpreter, thus dragging
her, willing or not, into the performance. Ruth-Ann understands
that commedia is essentially improvisational, but she stresses
that the interpreter should have been left out of it, period. The
interpreter ceased, at that moment, to be an interpreter and
became instead a kind of prop, a situation that prevented her from
being the unbiased conduit of communication, which is her sole
function as an interpreter. As Mac's Deaf Ed Department sometimes teaches, interpreters are *equipment.* They should receive no
more notice, when working, than their technological double, the
telephone.

Bob and Diane point out that in a scripted production, such
a violation would be unlikely to occur because the interpreters'
performance, as with the actors', would be rehearsed in advance;
the interpreters' neutrality could only be compromised if the
actors broke character. Shortly after reaching this conclusion, the
meeting ends. One week later, Ruth-Ann is fired. Her dismissal
comes as a surprise to everyone, including Bob, and her involvement with *West Side Story*'s development ends with just that single meeting.

Ronald Dorn is new to Mac, but he is among the most powerful
figures on campus. He oversees the business office and his
department handles all financial affairs, from expenditures to
paychecks. On February 20, 1999, Diane surprises him by

announcing that she needs his signature on a proposal directed to the Illinois Arts Council (IAC). On any other day, she would have approached Jim Goulding, the dean of the college, or President Larry Bryan, but both are out of town and the deadline for her proposed grant has arrived. Both Goulding and Bryan have been kept up to speed on *West Side Story*'s financial needs, but few others on campus are even aware that the project, still a year away, exists.

Diane does not look forward to ambushing Ron, but she determines that she has no choice; he is the only other person on campus with the authority to sign her application. She locates him in his office and presents the forms. Ron, scanning the paperwork, quickly realizes that he is looking at a 60-40 style grant, with Mac left to pay for an estimated $4,580 in production costs. Any overage in the budget will also be Mac's problem. For a financially strapped institution, $4,580 is not an insignificant sum. Diane, with a certain amount of contrition, admits that she isn't giving him much warning. Ron's terse reply: "No. You're not."

Nevertheless, he signs the proposal. In doing so, he automatically becomes a member, however tacit, of the project's eight-person steering committee, as stated on the second page of the grant application. The active membership of the committee never rises above five.

An $11,450 budget for a Mac theater production, however worthy, would have been completely unheard of just one year earlier. Mac's old theater building, last used as a temporary church, has been empty since 1984. The ministry that rented the building updated the electrical systems and the plumbing, but did neither to code, and when the ministry shut down, local fire marshals deemed the building unsafe and uninhabitable. Until 1997, Mac itself had not witnessed a faculty-directed theater production since 1982, when Phil Decker, professor emeritus, reluctantly allowed the Theater Department to merge with the English Department. Theater had been a three-person department for years, but attrition and budget cuts left Phil as the last man standing, and he chose to discontinue the drama program rather than soldier on with no help and little chance of living up to his own high standards. It was not until the mid-1990s that a group of students, working with minimal funds through the student-chaired Student Activities Finance Committee, began to mount their own productions, including *Butterflies Are Free* and *Black Comedy*. Noting the resurgent interest, the Mac faculty, led by Phil Decker, decided to create a position within the English Department for an Assistant Professor of Drama. Not long after filling that post, Diane clashed with the students over the student-controlled budget and over Diane's choice of material. *Antigone in New York*, with its ribald language, offended many students from the outset, and several students refused to even audition. Later, with the atmosphere somewhat cooler, one student confessed to Diane, "We thought you were just here to sign our checks."

In lieu of an actual theater, Diane inherited the dance studio, lined on two walls with full-length mirrors and a companion barre, still solidly bolted to the floor. The heavily waxed hardwood floor sported green and red painted lines left over from fencing tournaments, and the room, at first glance, had the look of a mispainted basketball court. Unpainted cinderblock walls culminated in a sixteen-foot ceiling with two lateral skylight systems. These skylights worked so well that they made daytime and matinee performances all but impossible. The studio space also included a main entrance with wooden double doors, a fire exit, a demolished drinking fountain, a bright red fire extinguisher, and two closets, one of which had been devoted to props and doubled as a minuscule greenroom (the space that actors occupy when offstage during performances). The other closet, until the late fall of 1998, held outdated audiovisual and athletic equipment, after which it became an all-purpose dump for the theater's lumber and building materials.

Lumber has, unfortunately, been among the nascent theater's most difficult problems. There is no place within the education complex, the facility that houses the studio, to stash it. Past student productions tended to overbuy, leaving increasing piles of unused and esoteric wood lying around the studio floor. These piles, together with a set of poorly made flats—both wood-faced and canvas-covered—joined with bulky, heavy props like a refrigerator and a dilapidated sink to completely fill one end of the studio space. The single most important factor in determining both the stage space and the seating area for any given audience has become this heap of theatrical junk, and considerable time and energy is spent rearranging it with each successive production. Throwing it out en masse is not a viable option, since there is insufficient money to tolerate any waste.

Despite the room's eccentricities, progress has been made. The college painted the entire space black (walls, floor, and ceiling) before the fall 1998 production, creating a proper black box theater space. The same workers, employees of Mac's physical plant, also covered the skylights. They routed extra power to the room, allowing for more lights (which, during earlier productions had repeatedly overloaded the circuits and pitched the company into darkness). They removed or covered most of the mirrors, along with the barre. Using simple two-by-four frames covered in Duvateen, a flame-retardant black fabric not unlike thick felt, students and staff created a system of movable, modular walls. People entering the space to see *Tartuffe* could not believe the difference. "It's like a real theater," was by far the most frequent comment. Like but not, apparently, the same. The studio theater still lacked a proper lighting system (previous shows had relied primarily on rentals) and any sound effects or music had to be routed through a single-disc CD player hooked into two monaural public address speakers dating from the 1950s. Each successive production had to make a choice between two equally dubious seating options. First, a stack of small metal chairs allowed for somewhat greater seating capacity, but the chairs were notoriously uncomfortable and many exhibited suspicious stains and obvious rust. The neighboring student union building housed a number of newer, more comfortable plastic chairs, but these had to be ferried over by hand on opening night and returned the night the show closed, a time-consuming and arduous project.

Thanks to a sizable donation from Amy Wolff Stein, a 1932 Mac alumna, the lighting system and the chairs were both upgraded in early 1999. A local company, Brent Lighting Systems, hung a proper forty-circuit lighting grid from the ceiling. They installed a forty-eight-channel dimmer board and a twenty-four-channel patch bay. New chairs arrived, padded and covered in purple cloth, just hours before the student-directed spring show of Moliere's *The Learned Ladies*. A technician added new speakers to the grid, together with the requisite amplifiers and a graphic equalizer. Going into *West Side Story* and its forebear, the fall production of Ibsen's *Ghosts*, Mac had, for the first time in recent memory, a recognizably functioning theater, renamed the Marian Chase Schaeffer Studio Theater. While not overly large, the space is extraordinarily flexible and more than sufficient, especially from ISD's point of view: ISD has no theater space at all.

With other Mac theater productions, no more than a few months of advance planning have been required. *West Side Story* demands a longer horizon, both for logistical reasons and because of the show's unusually high budget. Diane has not attempted a musical before, and aside from the difficulties that the music itself poses, American musicals are an expensive breed to stage: the rights to the libretto and score alone will cost twelve hundred dollars. Given the large cast, costumes (especially shoes) will also be a factor. The set, which ricochets from various streets to a soda shop to a dressmaker's store, in and out of bedrooms, and down to Manhattan's back alleys, will be complex. In a perfect world, money to pay for such expenditures would grow on every tree, but since it does not (at least in Jacksonville), Diane turns instead to the slow but rewarding process of applying for the IAC grant that she later presents to Ron Dorn.

The bulk of the IAC funding, which takes months to approve, is slated to bring and house Christopher Smith, a choreographer from the Chicago area. Christopher is a member of the Deaf community and is the only deaf artist that IAC has ever added to their list of eligible resident artists (which they did expressly at Diane's request). He comes highly recommended by Stephen Buescher, who met and worked with him while both were members of Sunshine Too at NTID. *West Side Story* will require nine weeks of rehearsals, and Christopher will need a place to stay during that period. The IAC grant is intended to cover these costs as well as his fee as an artist-in-residence. Diane has modified the grant application to cover one other position: an interpreter, who will need to be on hand when deaf performers attend rehearsal. Whether this role will be filled by one person or by a pool of interpreters who will rotate from night to night is not mentioned in the grant proposal.

Every other kind of production expenditure, from staples to glue to scripts and costumes, is Diane's problem. Her departmental purse strings remain tight, so a great deal of community support will be required to make ends meet. The grant proposal, which includes a detailed budget, assumes alumni donations of at least two thousand dollars, together with grants from other foundations totaling not less than seventeen hundred dollars. Ticket sales from the show itself will hopefully total $880, with the show expected to run for eight days over two successive Thursday-through-Saturday schedules. Privately, Diane hopes to funnel ticket income from *Ghosts* toward *West Side Story*, but she knows from past experience that monies generated by a given Mac department—theater in particular—do not always wind up back in the same coffers. Mac has many needs (the biology labs are a particular concern as of February 1999) and accounts get juggled to make ends meet. Diane finds this frustrating but freely admits that she has had tremendous administrative support, and thanks in no small part to Amy Wolff Stein's donation, Diane has generally received the funds she has asked for. The contrast between 1999 and her first weeks in her new position remains striking. When she first approached Dean Jim Goulding in 1997 and asked about her theater budget, he replied, "What budget?"

Christopher Smith has signed on, although communication between Diane and Christopher is difficult and, so far, slow. Telephone calls aside, and with Christopher still in Chicago, Toronto, and elsewhere, e-mail has been the principal vehicle for discussions between director and choreographer. The catch: Diane's native language is English, whereas Christopher prefers ASL. ASL is not, as many nonpractitioners may think, a signed equivalent of English. Instead, it is an entirely separate language with its own grammatical structure, syntax, and internal peculiarities.

Jumping from a visual language to a written language and back again reveals innumerable translational challenges, and nowhere is this more evident than in e-mail. In Christopher's e-mails, emotion takes precedence over standard English grammar, and many messages begin with typed exclamations of, "Oh, Diane!" He frequently sets these off in parentheses. One full sentence in an e-mail sent February 22, 1999, reads, "Diane (smiling)." It is ironic that many hearing users of e-mail have not adopted similar practices; after all, the impetus for such inclusions is the physical separation that e-mail implies. The addition of facial expressions or parenthetical emotions is not so much a "deafism" as it is an attempt to bridge e-mail's obvious visual deficiencies.

What Christopher keeps to himself is his fear that he won't be up to the task. Although he has choreographed many shows, he has only once attempted to coordinate a full production combining hearing and deaf performers—and that show, an adaptation of *Ain't Misbehavin'*, the story of and tribute to Fats Waller, had a cast of only six (two hearing, four deaf). In 1992, Christopher's *Ain't Misbehavin'* had a short but successful run in Chicago, moving from the South Shore Cultural Center to a downtown venue and playing to thousands of high schoolers, mostly hearing. One notable difference between *Ain't Misbehavin'* and *West Side Story*: every member of the *Ain't Misbehavin'* troupe was fluent in ASL, thus eliminating the constant need for interpreters and the inevitable delays in communication that will soon burden *West Side Story*. Anticipating this, even ten months in advance of the first auditions, gives Christopher pause. Will it work? Can it work? And if the *West Side* ship starts sinking, who will be sufficiently experienced to save it?

Jet Song

Because it is a low incidence handicap, the general public may not encounter many, if any, deaf individuals (those who are born with severe to profound losses). . . . Upon encountering a deaf individual for the first time, the hearing person, sensing a breakdown in the communication process, may first resort to shouting, hoping that the deaf person will hear them, and upon realizing that this mode of communication will not work, will attempt to discover if they can read.

Nanci A. Scheetz
Orientation to Deafness[1]

March 2, 1999. The revised body of the steering committee convenes for the first time. The basement of Rutledge Hall is warm and humid, and the English Department lounge, where the meeting takes place, looks tired and worn; much of the furniture, including the round wooden table that dominates the space, has lived here since the 1950s. A single blackboard competes for wall space with three tiers of unstable-looking shelves, and an old Gibson refrigerator hums and whirs in the corner. The refrigerator can be a major distraction to those who work or study here, but today, only two of the five committee members notice it at all, because neither Bob Dramin nor Paula Chance, a Deaf instructor from ISD who has taken Ruth-Ann's place on the committee, can hear a single sound the Gibson makes.

One interpreter is on hand, entirely for Diane's benefit, since everyone else present is more than fluent in ASL. Neither Paula nor Cara Hammond has seen the actual written proposal (mostly intended for the staff of the IAC), and the meeting grinds to a halt while they peruse the paperwork. Paula Chance would blend in perfectly on Park Avenue; her hair is spiky, with a hint of gel, and cut short. Her glasses positively sparkle, and she favors gold jewelry, an adornment she wears in plentiful supply. A loose-fitting maroon dress completes the picture, the sum total of which is forthright, bold, and eminently fashionable. Her equally flamboyant signing is full of broad yet definitive gestures and a certain hint of suppressed violence. Cara Hammond, by contrast, fits the Midwest. Her ears are triple pierced, and she often wears a bill-cap to work. She wears a conservative sweater with wide blue and white stripes. Her dark blonde hair does more or less exactly what it wants.

Paula can remember a time, not so long ago, when ISD had its own theater and a regular drama club to go with it. The state of Illinois ran out of funds during a crucial year when the building needed immediate repairs. When these did not get done, the building sat empty, crumbling, and by the time the school found the money to fix the original problems, it became cheaper to simply knock it down, which they did. Since then, ISD's few theatrical performances have taken place in Burns Gymnasium, which Paula sourly notes is "inconvenient" because the gym is in constant use and it's impossible to build a set or leave anything out on the floor. Every year, ISD requests the monies to erect a new, three-hundred-seat space, an edifice that Paula hopes would rival Sibert Auditorium, the crosstown darling of Illinois College. If it were built, Paula would surely be among the first to make use of it. She has taught at ISD for twenty-five years, and up until 1997, every senior class created its own play, self-written and self-mounted, under her supervision. More recently, she has scaled her efforts back to individual video projects, but she can easily envision a time when she could be dragged back into the arena of theater proper. Her last major foray was in 1987, when the Jacksonville Theater Guild invited her to direct *Children of a Lesser God.* She accepted, thinking in part that if she left the task to a hearing director, they'd likely botch the job. The show was a trial—the hearing actors, when signing, never aligned themselves properly with the audience—and also a roaring success, with every night a sellout.

As Paula and Cara review the proposal, Diane interrupts with a specific question. She wants to know whether "what's written on the page will work in real life." Paula spots Christopher Smith's name in the section for artist-in-residence, and asks if Christopher knows sign language. When Diane explains that Christopher is deaf, the level of enthusiasm around the room rises instantly, mixed, it seems, with a certain palpable relief.

Cara, who is hearing, speaks and signs simultaneously, and she brings up a litany of logistical hurdles, beginning with the overscheduling endemic at ISD. Most ISD high schoolers participate in athletics, and even those who don't, tend to have schedules full up with other activities. Cara refers to the few students who have extensive free time as "low functioning." In the spring, in the middle of *West Side Story*'s projected rehearsals, ISD has basketball and later, track and field. An eight-week commitment (really nine, including spring break) will be a significant hardship. Paula suggests letting the high school know about the project immediately, with specific dates, so that interested students can plan accordingly. Diane, however, does not have final dates in stone, partly because she has yet to see Mac's calendar for the 1999-2000 academic year. Cara also worries that Mac's breaks and ISD's will not mesh, and brings up ISD's frequent and mandatory "home weekends," where the entire school empties and sends the students back to relatives and guardians. Rehearsals, she says, absolutely cannot take place then. This obviates any and all weekend rehearsals. Paula recommends Monday through Thursday rehearsals, but Diane says firmly that this is not enough time and counters with Sunday through Thursday. Unfortunately, given the home weekends, this, too, seems unworkable, and Diane falls back on her more traditional rehearsal schedule of Monday through Friday. She notes that Mac students "complained initially, but they got used to it." She believes ISD's high schoolers will have the same reaction.

The total pool of high schoolers also becomes an issue. ISD has only 150 high school students. Thus, it isn't simply their heavy schedules that make their inclusion difficult, it's their talent level. One hundred fifty is not a large number to sift through when in search of a likely Maria or Anita. When the committee suggests that auditions be opened to younger students, Diane refuses. It's hard enough, she says, to work with high-school-age actors. Anyone younger would simply be, well, too young. As for including the younger kids in the project, the IAC grant demands that Christopher Smith work with all of ISD's grade levels during the rehearsal process, involving them in dance study, performance routines, and various activities that will, despite being unrelated to *West Side Story*, at least provide every ISD child with some direct benefit from his presence.

No one likes the various restrictions placed on the project by the IAC. Most damaging are the limits to the hours the artist-in-residence can work, a maximum of fifteen hours a week plus five hours of "planning time." Given that each rehearsal will last for approximately four hours, this seems to be entirely inadequate. Worse, Paula and Cara are quite certain that the ISD students will only be available, at least up until dress rehearsals, for just two hours a night, in a contiguous block from 7:30 P.M. until 9:30 P.M. The issue of how they will reach Mac's theater space presents further problems. Cara suggests hiring Mac students to ferry the ISD kids in newly purchased Mac vans, but in the end, Bob and Paula recommend making use of ISD's many adult supervisors instead. One thing everyone agrees on: There will be no excuse for absences. Either you're in or you're out.

The conversations weave haphazardly from place to place, facilitated at every step by the interpreter. Not everything discussed is relevant or even vaguely on topic. Whenever anyone cracks a joke, the resultant laughter, at least with Paula and Bob, is virtually silent. The conversations themselves are anything but silent. Both Bob and Paula inflect their signs with guttural punctuation stemming sometimes from their throats, sometimes from their tongues. Clicks and pops abound with, occasionally, the hint of a whistle; taken together, these sounds seem complex enough to form a living, viable language all on their own.

One sticking point is the notion of movement on stage, also known as theatrical movement, which the interpreter either mangles in translation or cannot manage because, perhaps, it has no real equivalent in either ASL or English. A discussion erupts over the nature of theatrical movement, and within about twenty seconds, no one has the least idea what anyone else is talking about. Diane, baffled, asks Paula to repeat her last statement, and Cara jumps in, attempting to help. Her clarifications only muddy the waters further, and Paula clicks her teeth with annoyance; she then launches into a fresh diatribe about movement, which once again, leaves Diane completely in the dark. Bob, if he understands, makes no indication either way, and the committee eventually abandons the entire topic as a lost cause.

A coherent plan does develop regarding the creation of fund-raising letters to be sent out on special letterhead printed with the following: "Performance Project 2000, a Joint Production of MacMurray College and the Illinois School for the Deaf." Some discussion over merging the two schools' mascots—a tiger for ISD, a Highlander for Mac—leads cheerfully nowhere, but everyone agrees to a deadline of May 1, 1999, for sending out the letters. Paula and Bob will write the initial draft and pass it back to Diane. With the official business concluded, the meeting suddenly perks up again, as if being freed of an agenda makes the whole process new and fresh. Paula has several opinions to offer, which she does in typically rapid-fire style. First, she has no faith in the dancing abilities of the students. "The football cheerleaders really stink," she says. "If we want good dancers, forget it." Moreover, she worries that the students won't be interested in the first place. She notes that "Quincy College has musicals and our students don't like them." She adds that at Quincy (a hearing college on the Missouri border), productions are "signed on the side," meaning the interpreters remain in a stationary position.

Diane doesn't believe attracting talented students will be a problem, especially once they understand that deaf and hearing actors will be onstage together. Paula, who is unfamiliar with *West Side Story*, has already found a new problem to wrangle with. "Deaf people—sharks!" she exclaims. Must the deaf actors be associated with what many people view as a man-eating sea monster? Diane assures her that it's not an insult that will transfer, even unintentionally, to the Deaf community at large, especially because "Tony and Maria are able to cross that boundary."

Paula remains unconvinced. The whole notion of gangs clearly rankles. "I don't want to promote gang violence," she says. "I don't want to have that."

Diane counters by saying, "If this play had a happy ending, then we might be promoting gang violence."

Paula shakes her head and gives the table a loud slap with the palm of her hand, a perfectly ordinary method, within the Deaf community, of catching a group's attention. She goes on to declare that the very act of separating the actors into a hearing gang and a deaf gang is divisive; whether they reconcile or not is hardly the point. From her perspective, the Deaf community has been ostracized long enough, and anything that might exacerbate the situation should not be tolerated.

Bob, who has been silent for much of the postmeeting meeting, breaks in with a concern of his own: "We must bring in an interpreter and that in itself really limits the communication," which will complicate efforts to demonstrate that the fighting between the gangs is wrong.

"We can't change the words," says Diane, but she stresses that the text is not all she has to work with. "We *can* change the spaces between the words." She reiterates that if gang- or violence-related issues need to be clarified, there will be ample room to do so in the acting and blocking of the final piece. Still, she can't help feeling she is backpedaling, on the defensive; she realizes she had assumed the group would be familiar with *West Side Story*. Largely because of this, she had not expected gangs to be a divisive or prevalent issue, and she finds herself caught off guard, only partially able to explain her faith in the stage as a mediating forum. Worse, her attempts at summarizing the play seem to raise more questions than they answer.

Paula changes tack and suggests asking Christopher's advice. After all, he is a member of an ethnic minority group (he is black) and a resident of a large city where gang violence is an accepted, if unloved, aspect of daily life. She goes on to say that "the concerns of the Deaf community" are essentially the same in Jacksonville and ISD as they are in Chicago and the rest of the world. Diane, uncertain how to take this, asks Paula if she knows the story of the musical or has actually read the script. Paula replies that she has not, and Diane, who had hoped to avoid the cost of renting scripts until just before rehearsals (still ten months away), promises to provide the committee members with preview copies as soon as possible.

What neither the interpreter nor Paula makes clear in equating Chicago and Jacksonville is the insidious nature of gang culture in general and its constant impact on ISD. Jacksonville's police department makes regular presentations to ISD's faculty, coaching them on signs of potential gang activity. ISD keeps a particular eye on repeated color schemes or students who avoid certain colors at all costs, along with specific hats and a vast array of ever-changing clothing styles. Neither the police nor ISD think that girls are often at risk, but boys who travel in packs are an immediate red flag, as are any sort of clandestine meetings. Paula remembers an ISD student from metropolitan Chicago who attempted to start a chapter of the gang he ran with at home. ISD responded by dismissing him from the school. Around the same time, a bevy of Jacksonville high schoolers attacked and beat a group of four ISD boys, apparently because the hearing group erroneously mistook the ISD boys for a rival gang. Given this alarming history, Diane begins to wonder if a reading of the script will be sufficient to allay Paula's fears.

As the group stands to leave, still talking, Paula ends the meeting with some caustic and not especially veiled references to the quality of the interpreter. The interpreter, still present and gathering his things, does his best not to listen or look, but he clearly understands. He escapes out the door as quickly as he can.

The issue of gangs in *West Side Story* stems directly from the text, for the tale follows two competing New York City street gangs, the Sharks and the Jets. The Sharks are Puerto Rican immigrants, and the Jets are white, mostly Polish. As first-generation natives, the Jets resent the sudden appearance of the Puerto Ricans in their neighborhoods. Riff, leader of the Jets, determines it's time to settle things once and for all, and he challenges Bernardo (leader of the Sharks) to a fight, a rumble. Riff recruits his old friend Tony to help, but Tony is reluctant; he's given up gang life for a job at a soda shop. Tony acquiesces in the end and accompanies Riff and the Jets to a local dance, where the terms of the coming war are to be set. Unfortunately for all involved, Tony meets Bernardo's sister, Maria, at the dance and the two immediately fall in love.

Not long after, at Maria's insistence, Tony tries to intervene in the rumble and stop the fighting. His good intentions distract Riff, and Bernardo takes the opportunity to stab and kill Riff. Enraged, Tony retaliates by grabbing a knife and killing Bernardo. Full of remorse, Tony begs Maria's forgiveness (which she eventually grants), and goes into hiding at the soda shop while they try to enact a plan to flee the city and start a new life in the country. Their dreams come to nothing when Anita, Bernardo's girlfriend, tells the Jets that Maria has been shot and killed. Reacting to this news, Tony comes out of hiding and is shot himself by Maria's Puerto Rican boyfriend, Chino. *West Side Story* ends with members of the opposing gangs joining forces to bear Tony's body off the stage while Maria and the play's few adult characters mourn his death.

The plot, then, is a barely altered adaptation of William Shakespeare's *Romeo and Juliet*, with street gangs standing in for the Bard's Capulets and Montagues. Given the absolute dependence of the plot and story on gangs and turf wars, the jitteriness of ISD's faculty is not without some foundation. What remains to be seen is how they will react after reading Diane's preview copy, and whether such a reading will be enough to quell their apprehension.

In the fall of 1999, just before the Mac/ISD production holds its first auditions, another production of *West Side Story* gained sudden and surprising attention. Amherst Regional High School, in Amherst, Massachusetts, made national headlines by abruptly canceling *West Side Story*, which was scheduled to be the school's spring musical. Under pressure from a group of parents, teachers, and students who felt the production showed Puerto Ricans in an unfavorable light, teachers and administrators at the school elected to pull the plug entirely rather than soldier on with what might have made for a controversial show. The resultant cancellation drew nationwide press coverage and probably caused more controversy than continuing ever would. In particular, the school came under fire for bowing to the complaints of a select few and thus, in the opinion of many critics, stooping to outright censorship. Many members of both the school body and the community at large were both surprised and offended. Still, when National Public Radio's *All Things Considered* covered the event, they found many students in full agreement with the cancellation. As one student put it when interviewed anonymously, "Puerto Ricans as sharks? I mean, come *on*."

Codirector Wendy Kohler had expected a certain amount of controversy. Over her long career at Amherst High, she had encountered opposition to musicals as diverse as *My Fair Lady*; *Kiss Me, Kate*; and *Fiddler on the Roof*. In each case, the objections centered around notions of stereotyped characters. Still, the vitriol that accompanied the selection of *West Side Story* caught her off guard. She had planned to mount the show in conjunction with discussion forums specifically designed to air charges of racism, something she had done in the past, but this time, faced with a petition signed by 158 students, she and her production team decided that standing on principle would achieve nothing. Citing her opinion that the atmosphere surrounding the production had become too poisonous to make a show possible, Kohler elected to go with *Crazy for You*, an adaptation of George and Ira Gershwin's 1930 *Girl Crazy*, instead.

About 10 percent of the students at the Amherst high school are Latino, and of these, most are of Puerto Rican ancestry. However, not all of the Puerto Rican students signed the petition; indeed, the community seemed split by the *West Side Story* controversy. One teacher at the school, married to a Puerto Rican woman, stated that the depictions of the Sharks were "vile," and simply unacceptable. Other students, however, saw the play as a vehicle for a more unifying message, one where love and cooperation ultimately win the day, even in the face of death and tragedy. The town and surrounding community seemed to agree. A rally held on the town common in support of *West Side Story* drew approximately one hundred people, including the ACLU, local aldermen, and state senator Stanley Rosenberg. Newspapers quoted Rosenberg as saying, "I think that denying the community the opportunity to see the play is wrong. It's wrong in a democratic society. You shouldn't seek to silence different points of view and that's what's happening here."[2] For her part, Kohler opined that the entire affair amounted to an assault on academic freedom.

Perhaps the controversy should not have come as such a shock, given the general story line of the play. According to some scholars, the basic plot line of warring families and star-crossed lovers dates to at least fifth-century Greece, although most would now identify *Romeo and Juliet* as *West Side Story*'s most direct progenitor. In both stories, lovers from opposing sides of a long-standing feud, the former familial, the latter ethnic, attempt to act out a romance despite the suspicions and ill will of even their closest allies and, in the end, one of them (the man in both cases, Romeo/Tony) dies for his trouble.

It was 1949 when choreographer Jerome Robbins first contacted composer Leonard Bernstein with the seeds of the idea for what would become *West Side Story*, and Bernstein later recalled that the show was to center around disgruntled Roman Catholics and Jews. The setting would be the Passover-Easter season, and Juliet, only later renamed Maria, would be Jewish. Romeo would be either Irish or Italian, and definitely Roman Catholic. Luckily, or so it seems now, *East Side Story* took years to develop, and, by 1955, Bernstein and Robbins had abandoned their initial concept. Citing "the whole Jewish-Catholic premise as not very fresh," they hared off in a new direction, that of teenage gangs, immigrants one and all, but with one side (the Puerto Ricans) a good deal more recently arrived.[3] Even then, however, the mood and style of the piece had not fully formed; when librettist Arthur Laurents suggested the title *Gangway!*, the others took it seriously and had it inscribed on copies of the script and sections of early scenery.[4]

The decision to feature teens melded perfectly with a nationwide trend toward recognizing not merely the existence of but also the social power of teen culture. From language to fashion, postwar America leaned increasingly on (largely urban) teenage attitudes, ideals, and idioms. In *West Side Story*, teen lifestyle could be celebrated with reasonable accuracy without breaking from tried and true dramatic—and theatrical—tradition. Hollywood had already shown the way, thanks to Marlon Brando in *The Wild One* (1953) and then, more explicitly, with James Dean and the stylish, melodramatic *Rebel Without a Cause* (1955, and costarring Natalie Wood, soon to star in the film version of *West Side Story*). *The Blackboard Jungle* (1955) added musical rebellion to the mix by featuring Bill Haley's "Rock around the Clock." All three films helped cement a newfound tendency to treat all teenage culture as synonymous with delinquency. Then along came the double whammy of Elvis Presley, who conquered both the radio waves and Hollywood (the films especially, like *Jailhouse Rock*, were unapologetically targeted at teens).

By the time *West Side Story* opened on Broadway in September 1957, audiences were primed and ready for a serious drama depicting contemporary teen life. *West Side Story* ran for 772 performances, nearly two years, then toured nationally before returning to New York and posting an additional 253 performances during 1960. Its creators recall something less than universal acclaim—Walter Kerr, writing for the *New York Herald Tribune*, was particularly savage—but overall, reviews were favorable. Still, the show did not receive anything like the unanimous affection it currently enjoys until 1961, when a film version

appeared starring Natalie Wood and Richard Beymer (later of
Twin Peaks fame). By then, the eccentricities of the music and the
somber mood of the show, so atypical of comedic musicals, had
grown more palatable, almost familiar. Once committed to cellu-
loid, *West Side Story*'s reputation was assured, and with rare
exceptions, it has continued to bask in a wealth of plaudits ever
since. One notable exception was film critic Pauline Kael, who
damned both the stage and big screen versions with equal venom
when she wrote:

> Consider the feat: first you take Shakespeare's *Romeo and Juliet*
> and remove all that cumbersome poetry; then you make the Mon-
> tagues and Capulets really important and modern by turning them
> into rival street gangs of native-born and Puerto Ricans. (You get
> rid of the parents, of course; America is a *young* country—and
> who wants to be bothered by the squabbles of older people?) . . .
> The irony of this hyped-up, slam-bang production is that those
> involved apparently don't really believe that beauty and romance
> *can* be expressed in modern rhythms—for whenever their Romeo
> and Juliet enter the scene, the dialogue becomes painfully old-
> fashioned and mawkish, the dancing turns to simpering, sickly
> romantic ballet, and sugary old stars hover in the sky.[5]

Bernstein, at least, would likely have been surprised to find
anyone opposed to *West Side Story* on grounds of racism or
favoritism. He was himself a practicing Jew, yet one of his greatest
creations was an operatic interpretation of the Roman Catholic
mass, simply entitled *Mass* (a production that served to inaugurate
the John F. Kennedy Center for the Performing Arts). In 1985, he
agreed to conduct an evening of Richard Wagner's music at the
Vienna State Opera, a city that for several years served as Hitler's
intellectual seat of power. Perplexed, Bernstein set about video-
taping himself in various Vienna neighborhoods, including at the
door of Sigmund Freud's old house. The tape began with Bernstein's own subtitle, "What's a nice Jewish boy like you doing in a
place like this playing racist music?" Given that the subject was
clearly on his mind, it seems doubtful that Bernstein would have

incorporated prejudice (knowingly, at least) into any of his work. It is Bernstein, after all, who once referred to Wagner as "a first-rate genius" but "a third-rate man."[6]

Nor does it seem likely that either Arthur Laurents or lyricist Stephen Sondheim (also Jewish) would have included any such message. Laurents, lesser known to the world at large than his fellow collaborators, is a true Broadway legend, a man whose theatrical interests overflowed into screenplays, novels, and directing. He wrote the libretto for *Gypsy* and authored the screenplays for *Rope*, *The Way We Were*, and *The Turning Point*. In 1984, he won a Tony for directing *La Cage Aux Folles*. Early in his career, he wrote radio scripts for shows such as *Hollywood Playhouse*, *The Thin Man* and *This Is Your FBI*. Clearly, Laurents was a man with formidable range and a willingness to take on potentially risky subjects (homosexuality in both *La Cage* and *Rope*, for example).

Even though Sondheim was the last of the four major collaborators brought on board (this was the show that made his name), the story and its characterizations fit his personal thematic concerns perfectly. Ineffectual or absent parents and adults litter his work, from *Assassins* to *Into the Woods*; his productions form a sometimes depressing canvas where even those who might be well intentioned tend to fail in the end. Perhaps unsurprisingly, Sondheim has described himself, not as an unhappy child, but as one whose parents, his mother in particular, took little interest in him—at least until his teenage years, when she attempted to seduce him. His lyrics for *West Side Story* suggest that he views the Puerto Ricans with great sympathy, and moreover, that he equates their plight with that of their "Americanized" counterparts, the Jets. From a turn-of-the-millennium perspective, it might be tempting to view only the Sharks as disaffected, but it is essential to remember that when Sondheim hammered out *West Side Story*'s lyrics, the nation at large would have seen the Jets and Sharks as equally delinquent and dangerous simply by virtue of their being teens. Both gangs lead derelict lives, bereft of parental guidance or even meaningful influence from adult society. Sondheim and Laurents take both sides, aligning themselves equally with both Jet and Shark, and thus with youth culture in general. The script further suggests that the teens' gangland conflicts only mirror the more repressed, buried conflicts that the adults wish they could act out for themselves. It seems that neither skin color nor ethnicity are the heart of the problem. What Sondheim and Laurents ultimately condemn is adult indifference, the kind of ingrained inertia and easy hatred that allow ethnic conflicts to flourish.

As for Robbins, he created more than fifty ballets over the course of his career (*Fancy Free, The Tender Land, Afternoon of a Faun, Dances at a Gathering*, etc.) and worked alongside many of the art's leading exponents, including Peter Martins and George Balanchine. The four Tonys, two Academy Awards (for the film version of *West Side Story*, from which United Artists ultimately fired him), and five Donaldsons are merely the tip of the iceberg in terms of public and critical recognition. One show that stands out is his work on *Fiddler on the Roof* (1964), a tale that depicts the plight of Russian Jews evicted from their village and forced to emigrate to points unknown. Like *West Side Story*, *Fiddler* is a show that relies heavily on the politics, both social and governmental, of repression and intolerance. In both stories, ethnicity defines culture and culture ethnicity. Working outward from this dialectical interdependency, Robbins created dances as tribal expression, as badges of pride. Thumbing his nose at Puerto Ricans was hardly on his mind; one look at the brilliant razzmatazz of "America," full of exuberant whoops and kicks (immortalized on film), should be enough to dispel any notion that he thought of Puerto Ricans as somehow inferior.

Amherst High was not alone in its condemnation, however. Indeed, before *West Side Story* ever debuted—in Washington, D.C., where it went for pre-Broadway trials—it met with an immediate tongue-lashing from the Puerto Rican community.

Sondheim received a letter expressing outrage at one line in particular from "America," in which Anita lampoons Puerto Rico as
an "island of tropic diseases." The letter urged Sondheim, on
behalf of all Puerto Ricans, to remove the offending line. He did
no such thing and, on opening night, Bernstein received a telephone call from *La Prensa*, the national newspaper of Puerto
Rico, warning that the Puerto Rican community would picket
the New York opening if the lyrics were not changed. The caller
informed him that everyone knew Puerto Rico was modern and
safe, entirely free of tropical diseases, and that *West Side Story*
insulted Puerto Rico and Puerto Ricans everywhere. In the end,
Bernstein and company refused to make any alterations. The
script, they felt, spoke for itself; whatever insults are present in
"America" are all delivered by Anita, a native Puerto Rican who
now looks down on her country—an entirely believable perspective, and absolutely true to her assimilationist character. Moreover, the production team felt that Rosalia, who still actively
defends her mother country, answers or deflects each of Anita's
charges. In secret, they might even have wondered why no one
bothered to protest the bubbleheaded Jet girls, portrayed across
the board and without apology as idiots. When asked to leave a
war council, Graziella, a Jet girl to the core, says, "We might, and
then again, we might not. I and Velma ain't kid stuff, neither. Are
we, Vel?" Velma replies, "No, thank you-oo, ooblie-oo."

The creators of *West Side Story* are vulnerable on one point:
none of the four is Puerto Rican. Not one knew the culture with
the kind of intimacy that a native Puerto Rican would have, and
thus all four, together with their work, remain open to charges of
racism, if not through intention, then through ignorance and
clumsiness. It may well be that the truth in such matters is always
relative, that the eye—and ear—of the beholder cannot be fully
dislodged, but such a solipsistic attack should only be mounted
with the utmost caution. Taken to its logical extreme, this sort of
creed, like Zeno's famous arrow, eventually consigns all ventures,

of all kinds, to the void. If only a Puerto Rican can write about Puerto Ricans, then it stands to reason that only a Pole can write about Poles—and, in the case of *West Side Story*'s particular situation, both the Puerto Rican and Polish artisans would also have to be members of gangs, hoodlums themselves. What to do if the subject matter then investigates the afterlife, as do works as diverse as *Hamlet* and *Angels in the Outfield*? Presumably, the authors would themselves have to be dead.

The fact remains, however, that the Sharks as a group receive notably less stage time than their whiter, more acclimated Jet cousins. Of the Puerto Rican characters, only Maria and Anita receive ample stage time in the second act, whereas the Jets dominate the most pivotal sequences, such as when Anita flees Doc's shop without delivering the message that Maria is ready to meet Tony and escape with him to the countryside. In fact, the male Sharks only appear twice in the second act, both times in passive roles: once in the ballet sequence for "Somewhere," and then in the show's quiet, heartbreaking finale where Tony dies in Maria's arms. In the Mac/ISD production, actors on both sides of the fence are painfully aware of this discrepancy—as is Diane. Despite her goal of fully integrating deaf and hearing actors, Diane cannot overcome the initial biases of the script itself. In terms of competing for the loyalties of the audience, the Jets have time on their side. They appear first onstage, they have more of their own songs ("Jet Song," "Cool," "Officer Krupke"), and they keep the plot rolling in ways that the Sharks (with the obvious exceptions of Chino, Anita, and Bernardo) never do. Thus, it is every director's challenge, when confronted by *West Side Story*, to keep the two sides in balance. And, to the degree that a reader or viewer perceives these discrepancies to be a racist or intentional slight, *West Side Story* will remain a problematic production.

Fascinated as she is by the mix of hearing and deaf actors in the Mac/ISD show, Diane has never had any intention of straying from the original script's intent of portraying gangs of Puerto Rican and Polish descent. Issues of hearing and deafness will certainly drive the production's specifics, but always from within the encompassing context of the Upper West Side as envisioned by Laurents and Bernstein and their collaborators. As far as Diane can see, there is no other choice available; again, as she is fond of saying, the production team "cannot change the words"—and the script's words clearly define the ethnicities of its (anti)heroes. The only real question is which school will portray which gang?

By mid-1999, Diane has arrived at her decision to turn the ISD students into the Puerto Rican Sharks. In a choice moment of precasting, she plans to build the show around the tenor voice of Mac senior Ken Roumpos. With that decision made, logic insists it would be best to keep his gaggle of Jet buddies as the hearing gang. Moreover, the steering committee has warned Diane that finding ISD boys willing to give up athletics will be a trial, but the committee sees no difficulties with recruiting girls, which immediately reinforces Diane's preference for hearing Jets, because the Shark girls have more stage time and more songs than their male counterparts. Finally, Diane will have the ISD students for just two hours a night (at least until dress rehearsals), as compared with four hours for the Mac students. Because the Jets hog the bulk of the stage time, it seems wisest to also give them the most time to rehearse. (Were Diane ever to remount *West Side Story*, she suspects she would reverse which gangs were hearing and which were deaf. It would, she says, be "less dramatically conventional." Since the Sharks are the most recent immigrants on the block, it is almost too convenient to have them also be deaf; if it were the Jets instead, the invading Sharks would instantly become a metaphor for hearing society, in all its oppressive glory.)

Regardless of which way around a director deploys the gangs, *West Side Story*, in both form and content, is the ideal musical to facilitate the integration of a mixed deaf and hearing cast. The text deals clearly with prejudice and oppression, indisputably lampooning both as foolishness, but the text is only part of a broader picture. Where *West Side Story* becomes a real departure from previous musicals and their attendant conventions is in its music and structure. Unlike most musicals, *West Side Story* (except in the film version) has no overture; it does not rely on a pretty medley, a prequel of tunes to open the show. Instead, it launches directly into the plot. Perhaps this was the influence of Jerome Robbins, who, as a choreographer, might have chafed at having a show begin with a complete paucity of onstage action. Perhaps this was Bernstein's doing, an attempt to launch the audience into his musical roughhouse jive without the benefits of an aural guidebook. Thus, when "The Prologue" begins, it is danced, not sung. No scripted words appear until the belated arrival of Officers Krupke and Schrank, intent on breaking up what threatens to blossom into a miniature war.

West Side Story's break from tradition cannot be understated. Compare it with the beginning of *Oklahoma!* where the audience sits through an overture and then meets the hero, Curly, meditating at the top of his voice on the virtues of beautiful mornings. Nor does *West Side Story*'s music skip from song to unrelated song, as is the case in *Brigadoon* or *My Fair Lady*— shows comprised of unlinked musical numbers dictated by the exigencies of onstage action rather than by some unifying impulse. By contrast, *West Side Story*'s characters gain recurrent musical themes that amplify with each use, building to dramatic peaks in a style far more reminiscent of symphonic scores. Although this might seem, at first glance, to apply more to a hearing performer (or audience member), it actually makes *West Side Story* a unique forum for signed communication because onstage signing can be developed thematically and built, sign upon sign, with organic cohesion. Each new vocal number, while different, harkens back to the previous piece, making it easier to develop a sign-presence for the show as a whole. Admittedly, it seems unlikely that any musical will ever be truly Deaf-friendly, but *West Side Story* may well be as close as any will get.

Something's Coming

It was the hardest show to cast I've ever heard of. Everybody has either to be or seem to be a teenager, to sing a very difficult score, to act a very difficult role and dance very difficult dances.

Leonard Bernstein[1]

It's April 13, 1999, and Jacksonville's gardens have shot toward the skies, powered by a sudden and unseasonable warm spell. The opening topic at the latest steering committee gathering is a University of Illinois-Urbana-Champaign production of Suzan Zeder's *Taste of Sunrise*, which was shadowed; both Bob and Diane saw it, but Paula and Cara did not. Diane found the shadow signing confusing, and Bob felt that the distance between the signer and his corresponding actor was problematic and caused parts of the play to be unintelligible. The conversation regarding *Taste of Sunrise* becomes lively, highly animated, and the interpreter struggles to keep up; neither Paula nor Bob are shy about signing at the same time. To clarify what's going on, the interpreter takes to beginning spoken sentences with, "Paula speaking," or "Bob speaking," as in, "Bob speaking, you can't have interpreters fifty feet away from the person they're supposed to interpret for. Also, different people sign differently. Watching more than one shadow signer sometimes means watching two totally different languages."

The high energy continues, despite yet another warm, close day in the Rutledge lounge. Diane asks if there are objections, politically or socially, to shadow signing, because despite its evident drawbacks, it seems to be the best available option. Neither Bob nor Paula express any intrinsic objections—they merely want to see it done well, with care and attention to the needs of its target audience. Paula comments that when she last directed for the stage, she had two signers onstage, one male and one female, both clothed entirely in black. Diane starts taking notes, and the conversation segues rapidly ("Bob speaking, no, now Paula speaking . . .") to a discussion of what shadow signing means for the set and costumes. Everyone agrees that a three-dimensional stage (i.e., not having all the performers on one level) will be essential. Also, lighting will be key. Unlike hearing actors, deaf actors (and interpreters) absolutely cannot perform in extreme low light situations. Diane explains that she and her technical director have talked about using scaffolds to ensure that everyone can be seen, and the group seems satisfied with this idea.

Steve Tavender, ISD's high school principal, makes an appearance midway through a rewrite of the fund-raising letter. He dresses neatly in a pine green blazer, and when he reads, he takes out gold-rimmed octagonal glasses. He is tall with dark, straight hair and a definitive receding hairline; he carries an air of easy authority, and everyone, notably Paula, reacts to him with respectful deference. He seems to know this, and doesn't overplay the advantage. Although he is hearing, he signs with an air of perfect relaxation, as if it were the most calming activity in the world. His speaking voice virtually never rises above a murmur; it's as if he's become accustomed to silence, so much so that his natural baritone now must be kept in check. He makes numerous helpful suggestions during the meeting, the first of which takes the form of a mild but apparently persuasive comment. Paula and Bob have once again brought up their worries about gangs in *West Side Story*. Specifically, they are concerned that the students will be enticed into acting out the violence in the script, internalizing it, romanticizing it, and possibly even forming their own gang. Diane launches into a spirited but flustered defense of theater as art, but then Steve quietly murmurs that he believes that even the younger students will be able to make the separation between what they see onstage and what they do in real life. "It's theater," he says, summing up. "It's *theater.*" No one brings the matter to the table again.

Steve Tavender proceeds to earn a second set of wings by offering to house Christopher Smith at ISD's dormitories for the duration of his stay. Diane, who had expected to raise several thousand dollars to cover the 40-percent portion of Christopher's room and board not included in the IAC grant, almost splutters in her gratitude. Steve says he'll have to clear the idea with the school's directors, but he foresees no real objections. With a single stroke, one of the greatest stumbling blocks on Diane's agenda disappears. When the meeting ends, she is still—just slightly—pop-eyed.

ISD's modern, brick high school is Steve's turf, just as theater is Diane's. Turf and territory are very real concerns for ISD, especially at the high school level. Steve knows each of his one hundred fifty students by name, and he knows most of their families. He knows their histories, their backgrounds, the classes they take, the grades they receive, the friends they've won or lost. He has seen some of his students arrive at ISD for prekindergarten schooling at the age of three and watched them grow into sophomores, juniors, and seniors. He knows their hometowns, and he knows that more than a few of his students hail from disadvantaged neighborhoods in places like East St. Louis and the South Side of Chicago. Despite his public disavowal of gang-related concerns, Steve remains wary and unconvinced until well into the rehearsal process, and a faint tinge of fear—that the whole thing will turn out to be deaf versus hearing and nothing else—lingers all the way up until April 13, 2000, when he finally sees the show for himself. Only then, with the staging and script clearly pointing to the original ethnic conflict do his concerns abate. His caution is understandable. Gang violence has taken the life of more than one deaf teen in recent years, usually due to misunderstandings. Many gangs employ hand signals as pass-words, a carefully coded argot, but they have little comprehen-sion of ASL or any other official sign languages. Occasionally, on seeing someone signing, a gang member misinterprets the activi-ty as a rival's code, and opens fire—too often, fatally.

Steve's territoriality extends, at least in jokes, to Mac. He is an IC alum who began his long career with ISD in 1967 while still an undergrad. In the course of attempting to self-finance his college education, he was told that ISD would pay a small salary to anyone willing to come and student teach, provided they then lived on campus. Although he had no intention at the time of making deaf education a career, the offer was too good to refuse. He has been away from ISD only rarely since, and 1999 finds him beginning his sixth year as high school principal. He insists, how-ever, that he's "not a paperwork kind of guy." He believes that his forte lies in escaping his office and working with students, one-on-one, in the halls and classrooms. As if expressly designed for this purpose, his office has two entrances, one leading to more offices where he can meet with other staff, and the other leading directly, like an artery, into the halls of his school. The walls of his office contain further evidence of both his style and his phi-losophy. Various awards and plaques. A shelf of compact discs. A framed black-and-white drawing of two little girls, drawn by his daughter. Perhaps the most telling is an enlargement of an old *Frank & Ernest* cartoon, in which two angelic petitioners approach God on the top of a cloud. "There's been a glitch down there," says one, pointing back to earth. "Life's not fair!"

Sporadic follow-up meetings stretch through the spring, but by the end of May 1999, virtually all work on *West Side Story* takes a hiatus as both Mac and ISD let out for the summer. In September, the meetings (and an endless barrage of e-mails) resume, mostly to iron out the nitpicky details of schedule, transportation, and budget. The fundraising letters wing their way to area businesses, and more than a few companies respond positively. With every contribution, the budget firms up, allowing the creation of the first light plots and design sketches. It is the proverbial calm before the storm: the key dates of Christopher's arrival and November's open auditions inch closer, obscured, for now, by the banalities of day-to-day (read: nontheatrical) work.

The summer of 1999 does bring trouble of an unexpected sort. On June 27, Diane realizes something is seriously wrong with her upper right leg. She has just finished a two-day ultimate tournament, playing with a team of players drawn from states as divergent as California, Arizona, and Michigan. Ultimate, often called ultimate Frisbee, is a graceful but grueling field sport where teams of seven players attempt to pass a flying plastic disc into the opposing team's end zone. The dimensions of the field are one hundred twenty by sixty yards, and because there are no real positions, the amount of running is extreme. Knee and ankle injuries are common, but Diane has no symptoms of either. Instead, it feels to her as if she is about to tear apart at the hip. A hip injury is a possibility she does not want to consider; she suffered a hairline fracture in the same hip only two and a half years before and spent six weeks (in a fourth-floor walk-up apartment) on crutches. Unfortunately, a battery of doctors can locate no specific problem, and despite a total cessation of physical activity, Diane's condition only worsens as July drags on. A surly orthopedist issues a new pair of crutches, and Diane limps through the summer heat—and the annual Association for Theatre in Higher Education conference, in Toronto—with an increasing field of pain that now threatens to envelop the entire right side of her body. She nearly cancels a planned trip to Washington, D.C., to visit her brother, but at the last minute, she decides to take the plunge and go. Her situation deteriorates further once there;

while touring the National Museum of African Art in a wheel-chair, she has a near-fainting episode and the pain, far from ebbing, continues to grow and spread.

Back in Springfield, a battery of tests rules out the most threatening possibilities for Diane's sudden collapse, including lupus, rheumatoid arthritis, and cancer. X rays come up inconclusive, as do MRIs of her lower back and hip. Blood tests show nothing out of whack. Bursitis of the hip (a bruising of the bursa, a fluid sac surrounding the joint) seems to be one culprit, but no one believes that bursitis could cause her to lose the feeling in her fingers and toes, nor does it seem likely that bursitis would explain the regular yet transient pain that flickers across the entire right side of her body. Meanwhile, the symptoms come and go, and the doctors, one after another, ask the same series of questions and proceed through the same basic physical exam, probing mobility here, testing reflexes there. Diane's summer free time begins to run down; Mac's orientation week is just around the corner, and still no one has a solution.

The answer, such as it is, turns out to be fibromyalgia syndrome (FMS). No one, including the bulk of the medical establishment, wants to formally accept this "wastebasket" syndrome (it's defined not so much by what it is but by chronic muscular-skeletal pain that can't be explained any other way, thus making fibromyalgia a diagnosis of last resort). Nonetheless, when a local rheumatologist flatly states that FMS is indeed the problem, the obviousness of it seems beyond question.

The diagnosis proves to be both good and bad news. For some individuals, FMS is completely and totally debilitating. It can enjoy the severity of acute arthritis or fatal lupus. It can leave its victims mentally and physically wasted, bedridden, and drained. Also, because doctors have been slow to grant it official recognition, treatments are haphazard at best and generally boil down to stretching regularly, exercising as much as possible, and reducing stress.

FMS has been kicking around under a variety of names since about 1812, a year of both wars and overtures. Since then, FMS' regular shifts in nomenclature have contributed to its largely being ignored by both the medical establishment and by the populace in general. Worse, because the symptoms of FMS are generic, it has proven astonishingly easy to simply write them off as being due to actual hysteria. Brain dysfunction. Neuroses. Personality disorders. In literature, this is the territory of Charlotte Perkins Gilman's "The Yellow Wallpaper," a Victorian short story tracing the nervous decline of a woman whose husband is so convinced that she has a disorder that he locks her in a room dominated by yellow wallpaper. Once imprisoned, she rises to the level of her husband's expectations and goes insane. (The story was recently adapted for the stage by a friend of Diane's, Jennifer Blackmer.)

FMS is a disease that slips easily through the cracks of public perception. Fully 75 percent of those diagnosed with FMS are women. Most are older than Diane, but onset often occurs early and goes undetected (or shrugged off) for years. FMS tends to manifest itself in women under stress, with histories of depressive tendencies, and some sources claim that 26 million Americans currently suffer from FMS. Other sources trumpet that half of postmenopausal women are FMS victims and that most never know it. In younger women, a sudden and acute injury, often in conjunction with stress, tends to serve as a trigger. Depression— sometimes mild, sometimes severe—often waits in the wings, and Diane's rheumatologist notes that this should hardly be surprising, since chronic, undiagnosed pain will make just about anyone depressed. She orders Diane to relax at all costs and prescribes a series of pain medications, all ineffective. Still, a diagnosis brings hope, and the academic semester progresses much as any other would, except that Diane moves painfully, with a pronounced limp, and ceases almost entirely to smile. Colleagues offer their sympathies but can do little more than lend an ear. Patsy Kelly,

Mac's chaplain, frowns as she watches Diane hobble from the student union into the education complex. "Diane moves like an old woman," Patsy muses. "It's terrible."

October of 1999 sees the opening of Mac's fall production, Henrik Ibsen's *Ghosts*. Throughout the rehearsals, Diane struggles to keep herself on an even emotional keel. Despite the endemic strain of production, her efforts pay off. Gradually, the pain lessens and mobility returns. Just before *Ghosts* opens, she makes a surprise announcement to the cast: she is pregnant. In June 2000, six weeks after the projected close of *West Side Story*, she expects to be a mother.

November 10, 1999. Only five men appear for the first night of the *West Side Story* auditions, and two of these, Christopher and Chuck Nash, are part of the production team. Chuck, a round, beaming man with a bushy beard and black, shaggy hair, is a graduate of IC and a former Drama major. He now works at ISD and is in charge of student life. He is hearing, and his involvement in *West Side Story* has grown exponentially due to a sudden illness that has forced Paula Chance to withdraw from the steering committee. Chuck, with some hesitation, has taken her place. The other three men present are students looking for roles, but none have particularly strong singing voices; not one can come close to singing the role of Tony. Worse, one of the three is Les Marten, a troubled student whom Diane initially cast as Oswald in *Ghosts*. Les dropped out of *Ghosts* less than two weeks into rehearsals, insisting that the material offended his religion.

Kansas-born Carrie Moore is back for her fifth stint as Diane's stage manager. She's a junior and a Deaf Education major. Outside the theater, she often lets her straight blonde hair hang loose, but when doing stage work, she keeps it tied back into a careful ponytail. She consistently signs when she speaks, something she didn't do when she first arrived at Mac, and she does so even when chatting to friends or fellow workers whom she knows are hearing. She breaks this routine only when she's frustrated (and she appears, to the untrained eye, to be so more often than she actually is) or when she's in a hurry. But, for all her eye-rolling and heavy, clearly audible sighs, Carrie is a fine and competent stage manager, organized and diligent, eager to please. After each show, she swears she'll never do it again. Then, with each new audition process, she returns, like a bird migrating back from a long winter's respite.

Much of Carrie's grumbling stems from a somewhat fanatical work ethic and an overstuffed schedule. Just before Mac's 1999 Christmas break, Carrie looks at her spring calendar and fires off an e-mail to Diane:

> I figured it up last night . . . each day I will have twelve hours worth of scheduled, required activities (on average). That leaves me eight hours to sleep and four hours to do homework, get around, drive to and from places, and hang out with friends. I think that's adequate! (grin)

Time notwithstanding, Carrie often arrives early to the theater, not merely to sweep the floor—a daily requirement of her job—but to sit quietly and do as little as possible while listening to bands like Savage Garden or Vitamin C over the theater's new sound system. She also carries a selection of homemade CDs, mixes labeled not by the artists or song titles, but by mood. The CD identified as "Mellow" finds its way into the changer most often. Carrie refuses to eat the unofficial national food of theater workers (pizza), citing a distrust of cheese. When people make fun of her for spurning a newly arrived slice, hot and savory, she finally makes a concession, wailing, "Look, I eat the crusts!"

Terri Benz, a lifelong resident of Jacksonville, sits at the recently tuned but still off-key piano, an old upright that didn't even have pedals until the previous week. She is a 1983 Mac graduate, a Voice major, and Piano minor. She learned both piano and organ from her advisor, Jay Peterson, who still serves as the college's resident music guru. It is Jay who, after reading over the score and concluding that Jacksonville did not have the instrumental talent to provide a proper orchestra, gave Terri's name to Diane. Diane, who was cautious and diplomatic with Terri during their initial telephone call, had no idea how easily she'd hooked her. Even with nothing to go on but the most primitive description of the project, Terri knew she wanted to take the job. "I said, 'Oh, this is cool,'" she remembers. "Diane told me, 'Jay Peterson said you're the one,' and there was no need to think. I told her, 'I just want to see how you're going to pull this off.'"

Terri has never given up either performing or teaching. She serves as music director at Centenary Methodist, a church that sits adjacent to Mac president Larry Bryan's home and across from a monument carver specializing in headstones. As a mother of three, she has precious few free moments, but she still finds the time to teach piano to dozens of Jacksonville youngsters, and her reputation is strong. She keeps her thick brown hair on top of her head and off her neck; she opts most often for casual slacks or a knee-length skirt. Although it's not immediately apparent, Terri has the patience of the proverbial saint, and no one involved in *West Side Story* remains more cheerful and dedicated from one end of the project to the other. Her smile is easy, unforced, and the simple act of sitting down at the ivories is obviously a tremendous pleasure.

The vocal auditions begin. Whenever a student sings, Christopher leans into the edge of the piano so he can feel the rhythm of the music vibrating through the wood. Melanie Jacobson, Mac's visiting choral director and voice instructor, flits from the piano to a seat at Diane's right shoulder. She whispers her opinions to Diane as the actors read or sing their lines, and when students falter, not knowing the tune well enough to continue, Melanie bolts up and joins them, adding her strong alto until they've learned the part well enough to tackle it on their own.

Melanie cannot decide whether or not she wants to be involved in *West Side Story*; she has more than enough to do just finishing up her Ph.D., and her very presence at Mac is something of a surprise. Midway through the summer of 1999, the incumbent choral director, David Barr, tendered his resignation, a move that stunned Diane. She and David had already held several meetings, including one at her home, over dinner, to discuss *West Side Story*, and David had expressed enthusiasm for his role as voice coach and music director. When he left, he did not bother to inform Diane, and the first she heard of his departure was in August, with only weeks to go before the start of the fall semester. It was, she remembers, a devastating blow.

Having signed a one-year contract, Melanie's tenure at Mac will end after the 1999-2000 school year. Her long-term goals center around the choir, its health and longevity; she has limited time and little incentive to cultivate a perfect working relationship with other departments, Drama included, especially when that department (Diane) is about to sap her best singers, distract them from choir and potentially overwork their voices. Melanie is a trim woman in her forties, bold and sometimes brassy, a woman who loves to hold the floor and laughs at the slightest provocation. When she laughs, she snorts; when she sings, anyone in earshot understands that, with regard to music and vocal technique, she knows of what she speaks.

The surprise of the evening is not the lack of men. Diane has expected this problem from the first, and by the end of the night, she has reconciled herself to advertising throughout the community and all the way to Springfield in search of a tenor who can handle Tony's difficult part. Instead, the real revelation is the singing ability of sophomore Meredith Blair, a woman whose punk haircut and constant animation cause her to be pegged by virtually the entire production team as Anybodys, the street gang girl who desperately wants to be a Jet. In any other production, hard choices would have to be made, since Meredith also sings the role of Anita with real verve and conviction. Here, however, because a deaf student from ISD will act the role of Anita, Meredith winds up with two roles: Anybodys, as predicted, as well as the singing and speaking voice of Anita.

The need for voices rather than leading actors allows for intriguing casting choices in choosing Maria. Dawn Williams is a flexible, willing actor, but the range required for Maria—high F, well above the staff—is beyond her. However, when given the stage direction of, "I want you to read your lines as if you really have to pee," Dawn is the only woman who transforms her words into urgency without resorting to overwrought, cross-legged whining. Someone proposes that Anna Poplett could handle the singing voice of Maria, leaving Dawn to deliver her spoken lines. Nothing, however, is set in stone; callbacks are still in the offing.

Nobody knows yet where these disembodied voice-actors will stand, or how visible they will be. The discussions spring spontaneously from the casting and, as actors file in and out, all sorts of ideas come flying. Melanie suggests that the singers wear all black clothing and hide in the wings. Someone wonders if the singers can stay above the other actors, somewhere up high, like angels. There is some discussion of placing the singing actors and the deaf actors back-to-back, so the deaf actors can feel the vibrations of the music and keep pace with their signing accordingly.

Everyone is disappointed that auditions don't draw a better turnout. There are barely enough women to cover the basic roles, much less to fill in as the Jets' girlfriends. Still, Terri's excellent piano playing and her easy rapport with the students, combined with the fine vocal performances of those who do show, infuses the room with confidence, energy, an air of possibility. Nobody wants to leave. The production team mills around for a half hour and more, talking, wondering, plotting, planning.

Melanie, collapsed in a chair, confesses, "I love this space. I love being in here."

Auditions continue the next night, this time with the ISD students included. Rumor in the high school has it that a band of students might throw over athletics in favor of dancing and acting in *West Side Story*. The spark that prompts this minor but significant revolution turns out to be Christopher Smith. Several students have worked with him before and can't wait to do so again. This is hardly surprising. Christopher is an elf, a short man with a twinkle in his eye and an aura of energy held, just barely, in check. His posture is excellent and his chin is always up, at attention, ready to strike an onstage pose. For dance rehearsals, he favors navy blue T-shirts, very tight, together with deep red athletic shorts or sweatpants; he often removes his shoes and performs routines in cheap white cotton socks. He carries his gear in a fat heavy-gauge canvas backpack, olive drab and army style, frayed and worn.

On the night before the first auditions, Christopher and Bob Dramin, together with Terri Benz and Carrie Moore, gathered for a quick, buffet-style dinner at Diane's house. Diane and Christopher met for the first time at the front door, and Christopher could barely wait for the screen to open before engulfing Diane in a bear hug. He spent more time signing than eating during the meal, as did Carrie, who constantly abandoned her fork to serve as interpreter. When Christopher finished with his meal, he signed, with fantastic effect, that he was full, full up to his chin, full not just with food but with "the work," the work meaning *West Side Story*, and the actors and production space he was about to see for the first time.

Christopher makes frequent use of his voice. He can hear a little with a hearing aid or with headphones, but neither gives him a clear idea of what his own instrument sounds like; in a hearing person, his voice would strike many as stemming from a supremely unhappy individual. Although some words come clear, others strain out in a high, keening pitch; if you didn't know who was speaking you might, from across the room, think that some-one had suffered a painful injury. Christopher, like many deaf people who speak, is highly sensitive about his voice; he wants it to be more than intelligible, he wants it to sound *right*. Still, he is realistic. He claims he understands 50 percent of what hearing people say to him and guesses that, when he speaks in turn, at least 50 percent of what he says is completely misconstrued.

The dance auditions proceed with difficulty. Christopher, despite having a well-rehearsed eight-measure sequence to try with the students, has trouble coordinating his finger-snapping with Terri's piano. The "Jet Song" relies on syncopation for its effects, and Christopher can't quite get the alternating beats of step-snap-step-snap. Melanie finally bows to necessity and becomes both conductor and metronome; she stands downstage and, using heavily exaggerated movements, keeps Christopher on the beat. By the time of the ISD callbacks a few nights later, this entire approach has taken on overwhelmingly political ramifica-tions. No one questions Christopher's ability to "sync up" given more time and practice, but the high schoolers from ISD do not inspire equal confidence. The questions rage. Do they need a bass drum to keep them on track, something big enough so that they can feel the vibrations through the floor? What about hav-ing a hearing student dance with them, to give them something to follow? Diane remains adamant that this sends the wrong mes-sage, that deaf kids can't do it for themselves and need help. Instead, the ISD dancers will just have to learn it by rote. In per-formance, any help they receive will have to come from them-selves, from Terri, or possibly from lighting cues. They will not be led by hearing dancers.

But on this, the first night of dance auditions, perfection is hardly the issue. Just learning the steps—which, despite their brevity, are not especially simple—is more than difficult enough. The Mac students arrive first, and for almost an hour and a half, they run through the same eight measures, stalking the stage as menacing Jets while doing their best not to trip over their partners. The space is tight. At the Student Theater Association's request, the side curtains from *Ghosts* have been left in place for an upcoming Christmas pageant, and when dancers on stage right get to the end of their routine, they have a tendency to plow through the curtains and vanish offstage. Several new faces appear: two women and two men. The cast swells. By the end of the evening, only two non-adult hearing parts of any size remain to be found: Riff and Tony.

The ISD students flood in all at once just before eight. Arriving as they do with no less than five adult escorts, they bear some ironic resemblance to a gang of juvenile offenders let out for a weekend fair. Indeed, their instructors remain at their sides throughout the evening, and when the students spill out into the hall, as they do whenever they have downtime or the auditions get split into two arenas, a few of their escorts follow, just to be sure they don't melt into the night or somehow mix it up with the college kids. Overall, the ISD students are boisterous, very physical, and bracingly loud. Many vocalize freely and some speak. They trip casually over chairs and drop their coats and bags as if abandoning them; when walking, they tend to stomp or scuff. On the echoing wooden platforms used for the audience seating, this makes quite a racket. Their gestures magnify as befits the size of the group and so, when signing, they sign broadly, as if to cover everyone in view.

What is clear from the get-go is that the ISD students can't wait to get onstage and outperform their Mac counterparts who, as their auditions wind down, have "gone about as far as they can go" with Christopher's steps. Divided now into groups, they count off, snap, step low and lively, advance on the audience, rise, whirl, and then retreat, still glaring. Not everyone is equally adept—a few are downright clumsy—but the progress is evident. The auditions are clearly serving their purpose.

When the ISD students—all seventeen of them—finally take the stage, the space gets really crowded. The situation only worsens as Christopher takes them through their paces. Even with Melanie subsumed by her role as human metronome—she half conducts, half claps her way through each routine—most of the ISD kids can't find the offbeat. For some, it appears to be a completely foreign concept. Eventually, Christopher sends half of the group to another room to work with Diane on line readings. Before they go, he promises that they too will get a second shot with the somewhat emptier stage. Terri, who has been home sick for most of the day, doesn't get any kind of break; she's now played the same basic eight bars—sometimes only getting through the first few notes before a false start demands a reset— at least fifty times. Olivia Frome, an ISD junior with a mass of cornrowed hair and a reputation for hearing just about anything she wants to, suddenly yells in frustration, "People are clapping on the beat, not off! All these deaf kids are messing me up!"

From her seat in the third row, Cara Hammond yells back, "Maybe you shouldn't have so much hearing!"

The army from ISD departs at 9:30, nervous that they won't be cast and that Diane won't remember their names. Now the tough part begins. With Carrie Moore and assistant stage manager Nathan Grieme (a sophomore Education major), Diane, Christopher, Melanie, and Terri pull their chairs into a circle at the front of the stage and try to make sense of the panoply of faces. Carrie interprets for Christopher as needed. Most of the decisions make themselves, but choosing the voice of Maria will demand callbacks. Anna and Dawn remain neck and neck, and the certainty of the previous night's decision to split them between singing and acting lines no longer seems so obvious.

Christopher has little to add to opinions regarding the vocal performances per se, but he is quick and perceptive about the posture and expressions of the singers. Dawn and Meredith impressed him with their ability to physicalize the notes of the songs, but many others left him uninspired. Christopher accurately predicts, without hearing a single note, which women will wind up with chorus roles.

Choosing the roles of the various Sharks from the ISD group proves much more difficult. Nobody, not even Carrie, who spends a copious part of each week volunteering at ISD, can put a face to each name. A few, however, stand out. In short order, Charles Johnson (CJ) lands the role of Bernardo, the charismatic leader of the Sharks. The role of Chino goes to Joey Gillis, a tall boy with a shock of bleached Billy Idol hair who couldn't possibly pass for being Puerto Rican even with the best tan of his life. It will be his job to love and defend Maria—and then kill Tony. Olivia Frome will likely play Anita. She has the right sass, the right hint of menace in her eye, but Diane is not willing to commit herself just yet. Maria, the plum role, remains unclaimed, and several names come up, including Pearlene Jo Theriot. The final verdict: wait for callbacks in both cases.

Sharks and Shark girlfriends get divided up quickly, after a discussion about just how many bodies the space—and the backstage space—can handle. Various numbers are floated, ranging from three members per gang upward to ten. Ten, however, simply isn't viable; a quick physical example using the members of the production team shows clearly that the stage will be hardpressed to accommodate even twelve (six Jets and six Sharks) at a time. Finally, Christopher singles out those who couldn't dance a lick, and the rest, fourteen in all, wind up with roles, however small.

The absence of an actor who can sing—much less act—the role of Tony remains troublesome, and the final half hour of the meeting centers on locating a suitable tenor. Nobody wants to canvass the area high schools—it would be a shame to have a Tony who looks too young—so the other, more hopeful course, will be to run ads in the Springfield papers. In a city of 110,000, surely there will be a young tenor somewhere who won't mind a thirty- to forty-mile commute.

The name Scott Corbin never comes up, because no one on the production team has ever heard of him. By the time Scott finally bags the role, Diane is desperate—and losing him just two months later nearly destroys the show before it can properly begin.

Dance at the Gym

I will have to focus on each dance numbers and will have to adapt because of combine with choreography-sign and dance. . . . I would love to meet with your music director to discuss the lyrics with deaf actors. Yes, it would be awesome for hearing-singer to sing beside the deaf actors and singer on the backstage, it is depending on the blocking, you know?

Christopher Smith
E-mail to Diane Brewer, 2/22/99

Christopher Smith is a man so replete with contradictions that he can be entirely baffling. He is a trained dancer, light on his feet, creative, and more than competent in his craft, yet he also has moments of extraordinary clumsiness. No cast member turns out to have less spatial sense than Christopher, something that would seem to be intuitive or inherent in most dancers, much less choreographers. Undaunted, he perseveres with boundless humor, charm, and more than his share of personal grace.

When Diane asks Christopher to choreograph *West Side Story*, she does so without ever having met or, in the traditional sense, spoken to him. Stephen Buescher's recommendation is enough to get the ball rolling, and for several months, the only contact Diane has with Christopher is through e-mail—a definite blessing for connecting the deaf and hearing communities—and the usual maze of TTY calls. The TTY, or teletypewriter, is a device about the size of a large desktop adding machine. It has a keypad for typing and a small screen where incoming messages are displayed, not unlike many of the fancier final generation of electric typewriters. A strip of paper, receipt-like, spills from the top of the machine, recording the entire conversation. Much like two-way radios, TTYs come with certain protocols, such as typing "GA" at the end of every complete thought. GA simply means "go ahead" and turns the conversation back to the person on the other end of the line.

Despite the barrage of e-mails, neither Diane nor Christopher have much sense of the other before meeting. They attempt to bridge the divide by sending each other their abbreviated personal biographies. Christopher's is entirely business-like, listing various productions in which he's appeared and the numerous academies where he's either trained or taught. He has traveled across the country with touring companies such as Sunshine Too, and has worked both Off and Off-Off Broadway in shows such as *Lovelost* and *Progress*. After studying at the Joel Hall Dance Studio and the American Dance Theatre of the Deaf, he moved on to teach dance himself at the National Theater of the Deaf. What Christopher does not include in his bio is anything that might pertain to his life beyond the stage. Only at Diane's repeated urging does he finally come forward and offer a small glimpse of a history that he prefers not to think about. "You can't change the past," he says. "I don't blame anyone." He writes:

> Regarding some cultural questions, for your information this is not my nature to discuss this issue and in fact you caught me off the guard. Because where I was growing up, I didn't learn sign til I was in Whitney Young high school where they had small deaf programs. I was growing up orally and some hearing trained. I actually learned in ASL generally when I came to Gallaudet University, that where I discovered my identity. I strongly supported ASL because we the deaf people in general live in visual rather

than english. But again, there are different levels of deafness just keep in mind, Diane.

His love of dance began while still in high school. Whitney, however, was and is a hearing high school, and Christopher was the only deaf student taking dance classes. He dealt daily with "bullies" and "a long struggling for identity." He recalls one particular class that included a difficult dance routine that he could not master, even after repeated tries. Christopher's teacher responded by hitting him. The memory still pains Christopher, but he takes a certain solace now from a favorite Frederick Douglass quote, "If there is no struggle, there is no progress." Douglass, speaking in 1857, referred specifically to slavery, but his words seem equally apropos today, not only for Christopher Smith, but for Deaf culture at large and the entire discipline of theater.

At the outset, Christopher works more with Terri Benz than with anyone else on the production team, including Diane. Even before leaving the November auditions, Terri and Christopher agree on a method of coordinating the dances in advance, so that the bulk of the choreography will be complete before rehearsals begin in February. Unfortunately, the system they arrive at simply cannot work long-distance. Terri first runs through the score, concentrating on the dance sequences, and based solely on her impressions of the dancer's capabilities, edits out large swaths of the music. She focuses on links between musical phrases, and, if a fresh motif develops in between two others such that it threatens to unduly lengthen the moment, out it goes. No cuts are made in the songs themselves, and all the lyrics remain intact. Diane, while aware of Terri's strategy, avoids interfering. This, she reasons, is precisely why she hired a music director in the first place.

For her part, Terri frequently wishes she had more guidance. She begins to imagine composer Leonard Bernstein and his team of orchestrators as "drunken sadists, staying up late at night, just *trying* to make things horribly difficult." The score is tricky enough as it stands. Revising it, whittling away and melting it down into a feasible, danceable length for nonprofessionals, proves to be a Herculean task.

With the bulk of the editing accomplished, Terri records herself playing through each edited sequence ("Dance at the Gym," "America," etc.), and then mails each as a cassette tape to Christopher, now back in Chicago until February 2000. Christopher, however, finds himself frozen, unable to work. The tapes, devoid of theatricality, devoid of space and human models, confuse more than they inspire. He can hear the beat, but not the mood of each individual song, leaving him deeply worried. He thinks that perhaps he has gotten in over his head, that this is more than he can handle. Even viewing the closed-captioned film version of *West Side Story* does not relax him. He has never before, as he admits to Terri and Diane only later, created original choreography for a show with a live music director. In the past, he has worked only with prerecorded music—music that cannot be altered, that has the predetermined and very strict requirements of a beginning, middle, and end. *West Side Story* also marks his first attempt to choreograph such a large group of mixed deaf and hearing performers (recall that *Ain't Misbehavin'* had a cast of only six). Overwhelmed, Christopher asks his mother, who is hearing, for help. With her assistance, he begins to make sense of the personality of each song, and ideas begin to creep in. However, when he returns to Jacksonville in early February, he has yet to work out the details, the actual physical moves, of a single dance.

When Terri realizes what has occurred, she understands immediately that her personal life, for the next month, will have to be placed on hold. She has already devoted long hours to vocal rehearsals with all the singing actors, often hopscotching around a complicated web of schedules to meet everyone's needs. A typical day in January 2000 has a 10:00 A.M. meeting with Scott Corbin, a run-through of "A Boy Like That" with Dawn and Meredith at 4:00, and a brush-up on "Cool" with the actor playing Riff at 7:00. She has fully expected to spend virtually every weeknight through mid-April in rehearsal (four hours at a shot, from 6:30 to 10:30), but now she has the added burden of assisting Christopher in developing the dances. There is no time to waste, for the actors are ready and waiting. Terri and Christopher begin daily afternoon rehearsals of their own, rehearsals that Carrie Moore or Meredith Blair join initially, assuming that Christopher and Terri will need an interpreter. Terri, however, knows a smattering of signs, and Christopher, as patient as ever, remains dedicated to using his voice to make himself understood. Embarrassed by her poor signing, Terri tells Christopher, through Carrie, "If I sign something dumb, like, 'Your mother is a cow,' you can assume that isn't what I meant."

Christopher nods and smiles. "O-kay," he says, choosing one of his favorite words. Under his guidance, the two syllables twist and stretch into something far greater than the word was ever meant to be; when Christopher says "Okay," it becomes a sort of blessing.

The private afternoon rehearsals move in musical fits and starts. Christopher, his hands on the piano, listens to each of Terri's edited sections and asks how many eight-counts each one translates to, then takes whatever empty space remains on the stage floor and develops corresponding movements on the spot. One by one, Terri's carefully crafted edits fall by the wayside as Christopher either shortens or extends virtually every one, adding steps here, subtracting there. Gradually, Carrie and Meredith stop coming to the afternoon dance workshops. Christopher and Terri have worked out their own system and syntax, linked not by any language system in particular, but by numbers. Counting—the metrical, regular counting of a musical score—becomes their default mode of expression, as in *a-one-and-two-and-three-and-four, a-one-and-two-and-three-and-four*; and on and on and then back, full stop, to the beginning again.

"O-kay," says Christopher, and he holds up a hand, lost in thought, a sure signal that he's thought of something new. Terri waits, watches, and keeps a pencil, its eraser worn to the nub, in easy reach.

Each evening, the latest steps arrive hot off the presses, for the official rehearsal and the cast at large. Christopher demonstrates each move, leaving little need for translation. Terri coordinates the counts—offbeat or on, start on one, come in on three—and when disputes or misunderstandings arise, Carrie or another interpreter leaps to assist. Diane watches from the front row of the audience, suggesting little, wondering what Christopher will come up with next.

Meanwhile, most of the cast has fallen into place. Eschewing formal follow-up auditions, Diane relies on memory (her own, in conjunction with Christopher's, Melanie's, and Terri's) to assign the many remaining parts. Pearlene Jo wins the role of Maria, and Olivia Frome, as expected, is chosen to be Maria's sister, Anita. ISD students Patrick Baker, Michael Nesmith (no relation to the former Monkee), and Jarrell Robinson fill out the Shark gang, with Joey Gillis and Charles Johnson remaining as Chino and Bernardo. Amy Dignan, Jeanne Kujawa, and Jocelyn Cleary receive parts as the Sharks' girlfriends. The Jets' girlfriends have also been cast, with Helen Brattain, Anna Poplett, Dawn Williams, and Jennifer Harris.

The male Jets prove harder to find. First-year Mac student Bryce Hoffman looks young and harmless, so he gets the role of Baby John. High schooler Charlie Smerz is cast as Riff, ringleader of the Jets. Richard Atkins, another community recruit, becomes Action, Riff's powder-keg sidekick. Dane Vincent, who shows up for the first time on the opening night of rehearsals, gets cast on the spot as Diesel.

Diane has already conceded that the many different Jets and Sharks will have to be combined (thus Dane Vincent will speak the lines for both Ice and Diesel, turning them into one person onstage), but she needs one more Jet (at least), to play A-Rab. Rehearsals begin with no A-Rab in sight—also no Doc, no Lieutenant Schrank, no Officer Krupke, and no Glad Hand, those four being the adult roles required in the play. There are gaps, too, in the ranks of the voicers and sign interpreters, leading those cast members who do attend the early rehearsals to wonder, with understandable trepidation, just what sort of future the production might have. Most jarring of all: with Scott out of the picture, the show again lacks a Tony, and without Tony, *West Side Story* simply cannot function.

Tony or no Tony, the first challenge in choreographing *West Side Story* proves not to be Christopher's difficulties with hearing, but with the space itself and the initial lack of a set. The black box theater at Mac measures exactly sixty-two feet, ten inches by thirty-five feet, six inches, with a few peripheral indentations on every wall except the west. Given that 50 percent of the space has already been reserved for the audience, Christopher's remaining allotment is an area roughly the size of half a basketball court. "Small," he says on seeing it, a word that comes out as a comforting sound, the kind of tone many parents might affect to reassure a child. In this case, it masks a certain disappointment—a disappointment that grows considerably when the set itself arrives precisely two weeks into the rehearsal process, on a Monday. Bar by bar, brace by brace, six scaffolds rise into the air: three carpenter's scaffolds, and three smaller, narrower painter's scaffolds. Christopher's available dance space folds in on itself and disappears beneath posts of rusty yellow metal. Over the next two weeks, the set encroaches further each day as sheets of plywood and oriented strand board (OSB) jockey to surround each scaffold, providing entrances and baffling sightlines. (OSB is little more than glue and wood shavings, pressed together, dried and cut into standardized sizes; it is frequently used in rough construction.) In the end, the performance space—not counting the platforms on top of the scaffolds—becomes a triangle roughly twenty-eight by twenty-five, with a hypotenuse measuring approximately thirty-two feet.

The black box is atypical for small-town Midwestern theater. In fact, it's an almost unheard of phenomenon, and Christopher's muted dismay is not unique among the cast. Proscenium stages are widely known, as are various modified thrust arrangements. Theater-in-the-round is not uncommon. The black box, however, is a big-city species, a style of theater raised on the exigencies of high rent and limited opportunity. For those unaccustomed to the many excellent shows done each year in the cramped confines of black box spaces, stepping into one for the first time can be an immediate depressant. The black box has no gilt designs, no box seats, no trap or fly space, no sweeping vistas, no chandeliers, no balconies floating overhead. All the romance—the grandeur—of Theater with a capital T is absent in a black box space. Black boxes are simply short, squat, and functional. Many directors and performers love them anyway, if not for their mythic power (they have none), then for their intimacy. It's no accident that black boxes are the home of underground, political theater. In a black box, the line separating audience and actor begins to blur as it never can in larger spaces such as the Metropolitan Opera House or, locally, Sangamon Auditorium, located at the University of Illinois at Springfield.

Performance spaces like Sangamon have come to shape, if not define, much of the debate in the Deaf community over appropriate methods of staged interpretation. In a large theater, interpreters and the audience members they target are likely to be far away from each other, often far enough that the interpreting cannot be seen well enough to be legible. One common solution is to keep the interpreters well lit, even in scenes that would otherwise be dim or dark. A second approach, widely adopted, is to color coordinate the clothes of the interpreter with his or her skin color. Thus, a light-skinned interpreter will typically wear black, or at least a black top; a dark-skinned interpreter, in turn, wears white. The goal is to provide maximum visibility for the interpreter's hands and fingers, and also the face, because ASL and other sign systems do not rely exclusively on hand gestures, but also on specific facial movements. Unfortunately—but perhaps unavoidably—the distance problem in large-scale theaters often proves insurmountable. Such theater venues are unabashedly, even exclusively, designed for hearing audiences, and the Deaf community has responded, predictably, by restricting its diet of theater. Why, indeed, should anyone attend that which is essentially unintelligible? Lost in the shuffle are smaller venues, black box spaces in particular, the kind of space where every seat in the house lies within spitting distance of the stage. For all the complaints that Mac's space engenders, it is the ideal forum in which to engage a deaf audience.

The complaints from the *West Side Story* cast—and there are many—go largely unspoken to the production team, who hear about them third-hand or in passing. Those who know the story line well are especially unhappy with the tiny space. Even after an early February presentation where the production team displays and describes a scale model of the set-to-be, many remain doubtful. The room simply doesn't look big enough to hold *West Side Story*. In particular, Dane Vincent hates the Mac theater from the first moment he crosses the threshold. "It's . . . compressed!" he thinks, trying to envision where the bridal shop will fit, how Doc's soda shop can possibly appear from the cinderblock walls. Later, he confesses that he had never even seen a black box space, let alone performed in one. Terri Benz, however, cozies up to the space as if it were a favorite piano. Despite a personal familiarity with the education complex from her student days, she has never set foot in what was then still a fencing gym. Her immediate reaction is that the space contains endless possibilities; she sees it as a blank slate, waiting for its text. More than anything Diane has said, the space convinces Terri that *West Side Story* will have to be experimental, not only with its casting, but with its staging. It's only after the auditions, once Terri has had a chance to assess the unpolished skills of the dancers, that she begins to wonder how they can possibly fit. And where, oh, where, will Diane find room for her piano?

Space considerations ensure that the most difficult individual scene to coordinate is "Dance at the Gym," in which the two rival gangs meet on supposedly peaceful terms for a neutral-territory night on the town. Supervised by a sad-sack social worker, Glad Hand, the dance proceeds peaceably enough until Bernardo, Maria's older brother, catches her about to kiss Tony. Tony, aside from being a stranger, is a former Jet—and he's Polish to boot, the exact opposite of the nice Puerto Rican boy that Bernardo wants for his sister. The dance ends in a shambles, with both gangs stalking off, primed and ready for a war council. Tony caps the scene by singing the enduring solo, "Maria" (the most beautiful sound he's ever heard).

Set changes in the traditional sense are impossible within Mac's theater space, since there are no wings and no backstage area. A single tightly focused ellipsoidal spotlight and a disco ball provide the segue from Manhattan's blacktopped streets to the gymnasium's interior. By aiming the pin-holed ellipsoidal at the upstage side of the rotating ball and then dropping the rest of the wash, the entire stage (but not the seating area) suddenly swirls with a rotating checkerboard of green-flecked lights. This becomes the only moment where the show makes use of green, and it serves as a cruel echo of the green fields and country living that Tony and Maria long to reach. Everywhere else, all that the

Tony (Ken Roumpos) and Maria (Pearlene) meet for the first time. Phil Fiorini, far left, provides sign interpretation.

characters encounter is rust and decay and the bluish nighttime glare of old and battered streetlights. Only here, for a brief moment, does the world of hopeful fantasy take command—and so begins the "Dance at the Gym."

Christopher designs the gym's opening dance for the Jets and their girlfriends only. As Terri plays Bernstein's modified blues-based walking music, the Jet clique embarks on a jazz-inflected stroll. They occupy only the left side of the stage, while the right stands empty, awaiting the arrival, only moments away, of the Sharks. When Bernardo and company make their appearance, the music slides into a less relaxed, more threatening mode. It not only fits the dramatic needs of the story, but it presages perfectly the upcoming tensions of space and timing, deaf and hearing, that make "Dance at the Gym" such a tremendous hurdle. Virtually every actor in the show (with the exception of three adults) is now onstage. Even with the explicitly reduced cast, this amounts to twenty-two actors—and they are soon joined by a bevy of interpreters, for both voice and sign. For a brief moment, after the dances are over and before Chino escorts Maria off, the tiny stage bulges with twenty-seven performers, most of whom, despite the available scaffolds, are stuck at ground level.

Diane allows Christopher almost free rein over the first weeks of rehearsal, stepping in or offering comments only when Christopher directly solicits her opinion. They check in with each other frequently, not only during rehearsals but also before, in Diane's somewhat battered 1990 Honda Civic. Each night, before rehearsals begin, she drives to ISD, where Christopher has been housed, to pick him up. As they drive through Jacksonville's old downtown district to reach Mac, Christopher uses his hands, his body, and his voice to discuss what he has in mind for the upcoming rehearsal. Diane, who has to keep her eyes on the road and at least an occasional hand on the wheel, does not always catch Christopher's drift as quickly as she would like, but they never arrange to have an interpreter join them. Minor miscommunications abound, and they frequently mime and fingerspell their way through trouble spots, but neither gives a second thought to altering or ending their conferences on wheels. These daily pre-rehearsal meetings are their only private time, the only moment where director and choreographer can guarantee a moment to work together one-on-one. The brief car trip rapidly becomes a period on which both Christopher and Diane rely heavily—all the more so because the reverse trip, from Mac back to ISD, is rarely Diane's responsibility. There is almost always someone from ISD present at the end of the night who can ferry Christopher back to his room, leaving Diane free to drive straight home and either prepare for classes, grade papers, or collapse.

Where face-to-face communication is impossible, Christopher and Diane continue to depend on e-mail. The speed and reach of the Internet are a stunning boon both to theater artists and the Deaf community. For quick notes and logistical issues, e-mail may be unparalleled in bridging the gaps between the hearing and the deaf worlds. On the other hand, for more subtle or demanding issues, such as reblocking an entire scene, there is no substitute for eye contact, for standing in the presence of those with whom you need to speak.

Thus, when Diane concludes that Christopher's initial staging for "Dance at the Gym" fits neither the script nor the needs of the audience, she eschews e-mail and approaches Christopher directly. His work thus far has been good and his dedication unflagging, but something within "Dance" is not working—a fact for which Diane, characteristically, blames herself. The solution, as she tells Christopher, lies hidden in the text, and they proceed to rethink all the hard work they've already done.

The "Dance at the Gym" is supposed to be a shadow of the upcoming rumble. Every move is posturing, a chance to outdo and outclass the opponents on the opposite wall. This is violence cunningly repressed as art. Glad Hand, the emcee, orchestrates the first joint dance as an icebreaker that involves the Sharks and Jets circling one another in a tense promenade, eventually winding up with partners from the wrong side of the tracks. When the partners prove to be unacceptable, things break down quickly and the two gangs retreat to their own sides of the stage-cum-gymnasium for the ensuing mambo. Christopher, thus far, has avoided overt hostility by having the dancers perform not for or against each other, but for themselves, almost privately. Each side forms two parallel lines, one of women, one of men, and the dance proceeds without even visual contact between the gangs. The future audience, meanwhile, will have visual problems of its own because Christopher continues to align his cast with the walls of the room (and the set) rather than with the thirty-degree diagonal of the seating area. The result: no one will be able to see the actor's faces, except in profile.

After Diane intercedes—two nights too late, she thinks later—she and Christopher conclude that what they've failed to emphasize is the dance as competition. Christopher thinks, pauses, and fixes his work on the fly. In the new version, only the principals perform the mambo, Riff and Velma from the Jets, Bernardo and Anita from the Sharks. The competition becomes externalized and even involves a winner, Anita.

The promenade sequence poses even greater difficulties. All the girls, Sharks alternating with Jets, take the inner circle facing right. The boys form a protective outer ring, also alternating, facing left. When Terri's piano picks up a soft marching tune, the two circles begin to rotate, walking in opposite directions. After exactly eighteen measures, the music stops and the two rings halt. When it works—which isn't often during rehearsals—each actor should find an actor of opposite gender from the opposing gang at his or her shoulder. Even for an all-hearing cast, this feat would require some repetition, a careful coordination of stride and tempo. Many of the deaf actors have trouble maintaining a rhythmic pace. Again and again, people begin early or late, walk too quickly or slowly, and end up too far from their new, unwanted partner, thus forming a circle filled with enormous ragged holes. On nights when one or more dancers are absent, the whole thing falls apart.

The problem of gender balance also causes problems, because the Jets will not allow Anybodys (Meredith Blair) to take part in the dance. This leaves the dance boy-heavy, and to compensate, Diane pulls Action (Richard Atkins) out of the dance group and tells him that Action, already disdainful and cynical, would never have any truck with such silly boy-girl shenanigans. Richard plays this up, giving high fives to his Jet buddies as they process around the circle, then ignoring or insulting each of the Sharks in turn. Anybodys's disgust translates into her leaping on top of an available milk crate and conducting her way through the dance, a physical choice that also allows the group at large to use Anybodys as a visual cue to begin and end the dance. Even so, every dancer has a moment where they have their back to Anybodys, and cannot possibly keep her conducting in view. Moreover, with Action *and* Anybodys on the sidelines, the dance is now Shark-heavy, so Diane plucks Anxious (Jarrell Robinson) from the band of Sharks and hands him a small set of bongo drums.

Drums, preferably "a lot of drums, big drums," have been a part of Christopher's conception for months, because deaf dancers often synchronize themselves to music by feeling drumbeats through the floor, but Terri and Diane, while supportive, have worried that too much drumming might overwhelm the songs, especially with only a piano to provide the music. Obtaining a large drum remains an option, but Diane hopes that a simple bongo will do the trick, if only because it's portable and takes up no more space than any other prop. She sets Jarrell on another handy milk crate under the lowest scaffold and asks him to tap out a beat to match Terri's piano. Jarrell, who has reasonable hearing, is fascinated with music, especially percussion, and during breaks in rehearsal, he can often be found at the piano, banging out chords and testing for himself the limits of sound. At other moments, he plays havoc with Terri's portable electric keyboard, creating a cacophony of strange, nerve-testing noises. He periodically vanishes to walk the halls, darting around like a human Superball. Whenever Diane calls a rehearsal to order and tries to figure out who is present and who is missing, it is usually Jarrell who has taken a last-minute trip to the restroom, or simply upped and disappeared, despite the best efforts of the dorm parents. As a bongo drummer, however, Jarrell proves to be as dependable as clockwork. Between Jarrell's tattooed beats and Meredith's who-cares conducting, the promenade gradually comes under control.

Communication during rehearsals is always frenetic, carried on in at least two languages and fed by a hodgepodge of connecting sign systems, gestures, grunts, and the occasional complete breakdown. Nor can anything be accomplished without first translating the script into some sort of agreed-upon sign language. What, for example, will be the Sharks' sign for themselves? What will they use to signify the Jets? In the end, every single line has to be translated into ASL. To effect this, Diane has the deaf actors pair up with Carrie Moore and other Deaf Education majors from Mac. One-on-one, line by line, they work out ASL translations that will deliver the spirit, if not the exact words, of the script. The cast retains the actual language of Arthur Laurents' script wherever possible, but ASL does not incorporate every English construction or word, any more than does Japanese. Diane guides the translators only when they cannot decide on the exact intent of a given speech. Laurents' fifties-style slang, much of which he invented whole hog, causes everyone fits. In some cases, where idioms or jive find no ASL equivalent, Carrie and the students resort to signing SILLY, VERY-SILLY.

For most of the ISD actors, ASL takes a backseat to their day-to-day linguistic preferences since many of them rely on sign systems other than ASL. Chief among these are Conceptually Accurate Signed English (CASE), a system emphasized by instructors at ISD, and Pidgin Sign English (PSE), a bridge language that has developed through contact between native ASL users and signers whose native language is English. Carrie describes PSE as "what deaf people tend to use around hearing people—it allows them to hold on to the signs of the language they cherish, but it 'waters it down' for (hearing people) because it stays in English word order." Many deaf people who weren't born into Deaf families or educated in residential schools will tend to use PSE, Christopher Smith among them. With *West Side Story*, the gaggle of languages turns out to be the cloud with the proverbial silver lining, because translating the script doubles as a successful team-building exercise. By the time the translation is done, the two groups, separated not only by age but by culture, have developed a surprising degree of trust.

Still, no amount of trust can instantaneously assist the Sharks with the actual reading of the script. Deaf people, despite possessing all the cognitive and intellectual abilities required for reading, often fall behind when measured against hearing peers. Endless studies have advanced equally endless reasons for this discrepancy, but the exact causes remain elusive. One hypothesis suggests that hearing children learn to read largely from phonetic experiments—that is to say, they have a large vocabulary based on words they have heard, so when they learn to read, they equate written letters with sounds and then they sound out the words, often with the help of an adult. Deaf children lack the ability to hear sounds, and so they have no way to make letter-sound associations, which impedes reading comprehension. Researcher Ronnie B. Wilbur concludes that:

> By the time hearing children begin to learn to read, they already have conversational fluency in their native language and can be taught to transfer this knowledge to reading. Deaf children who have lost their hearing at an early age do not have this knowledge; thus, they do not come to the reading task with the same skills in sentence formation, vocabulary, and world knowledge as hearing children.[1]

The upshot is that deaf children must learn written English entirely through memorization of visual signifiers, without the advantage of the mnemonic enhancers (namely sound cues) used by hearing children.

Many studies link language acquisition to what amounts to eavesdropping. Hearing children learn language and gain information by listening to the adults and children around them. Researchers concede that not all of what is heard is true or verifiable, but even the most spurious overheard talk increases a listener's overall vocabulary and information base. Deaf children, who are isolated from most of what is said around them, often have a more limited base of information. Thus, the greater the hearing loss, the more unskilled the reader is likely to be. A 1966 study working with a national sample of deaf children determined that only 8 percent read above the fourth-grade level.[2] Test results published by Trybus and Karchmer in 1977 covered a random sample of 6,871 deaf students, and revealed that the median reading level for a twenty-year-old, described in grade level, was only 4.5.[3] The same test reached a general conclusion that a mere 10 percent of eighteen-year-old readers functioned at above an eighth-grade reading level. A 1994 study conducted by Paul and Quigley (limited to profoundly deaf children) determined that ten- to twelve-year-olds read at a 2.5 grade level, that thirteen-to fifteen-year-olds read at a 2.9 grade level, and that sixteen-to eighteen-year-olds managed only a 3.6 grade level for reading. This study effectively reveals that the average rise in reading skills for profoundly deaf students increased by only 1.1 grade levels during that nine-year period.[4] Other tests reveal that deaf students proceeding from the ages of eight to eighteen are generally able to increase their vocabularies by approximately the same amount as a hearing child moving from kindergarten through second grade.[5]

To state that limited sensory and informational input is the primary reason for a deaf person's potentially weak reading and writing skills is a drastic oversimplification. The search for why deaf students underachieve in reading relative to their hearing peers has taken researchers down paths that begin with pedagogy and audiology, but inevitably lead to linguistic theory and issues of epistemology. The question of how we know what we know becomes substantially trickier when *we* does not refer merely to the hearing but also to those who must acquire language and knowledge through wholly different or at least modified means. As Carol Musselman writes,

> [N]o one knows yet how deaf children learn to read. And the jury is still out on whether they use processes that are qualitatively similar or dissimilar to those used by hearing children, for whom printed language is primarily an alternative representation of spo-

ken language. This is essentially the crux of the matter: Since few deaf children succeed in acquiring functional levels of spoken language, it is perhaps surprising that they learn to read at all.[6]

Research suggests that deaf and hearing students often pursue reading acquisition on parallel tracks. For example, both groups tend to use phonological codes (in which short-term memory converts print into a sound-based referent) to make sense of written language, and both groups "tend to confuse printed words that sound alike."[7] Both groups use orthography, the study of the correct shape of individual letters, to distinguish meanings. Students with higher levels of hearing will be more likely to equate certain letters and syllables with an accurate phonological equivalent, whereas students with little to no hearing must find other avenues for comprehension and retention. Recent studies suggest that deaf children encode (and thereby memorize) print through sign representations and that a high level of achievement in this practice can mediate otherwise poor reading skills.[8] This finding also implies that deaf children with a solid language base in the early years (such as those born to Deaf parents and immediately inducted into the use of ASL) will have a higher degree of success in learning to read printed English than will many of their deaf peers whose linguistic immersion is delayed.

Reading ability impacts *West Side Story* primarily at the outset, because once the English sentences have been translated to a sign system, the written text no longer serves as anything more than a baseline for the deaf performers and a common point of reference for the production team (especially the stage manager). Lines, however, still must be memorized, whether as sign or speech, and it takes several weeks (longer for some) before everyone is off book. Meredith, who understands ASL and CASE, has a distinct advantage in that she can cheat by glancing at Olivia, the actor she will voice for—provided that Olivia has memorized her lines in sign. Olivia, curiously enough, has the same advantage in reverse. Because her hearing loss is mild, she can delay her signing in order to listen to Meredith's spoken lines. The unexpected result of pairing these two is that neither one memorizes her lines properly for almost two months, because in completely inappropriate ways, each comes to rely on cues from the other.

Olivia's obstacles do not end with her voicer. Because she is exceptionally oral and has attended hearing schools for years (the 1999-2000 school year is her first at ISD), she knows very little of ASL and relies almost exclusively on Signed English. She picks up large chunks of ASL simply from participating in *West Side Story*, but mastery is years away at best, and there are moments when she has no idea what the person signing to her has said except by harking back to the printed script. The most confusing scene for her is her first, where she makes "a dress for dancing" for Maria (Pearlene Jo), and Maria, in Spanish, pleads for a lower neckline. Even in the final performances, Maria's Spanish-to-English-to-ASL signs look like nonsense to Olivia, but she covers her dismay by memorizing her responses—often without making appropriate eye contact. "You're supposed to be deaf!" Diane yells. "How are you going to know what Maria is saying if you aren't watching her hands?"

Meanwhile, inspired by their Shark competition, the Jets proceed to develop a sign system of their own. Whenever two gang members greet each other, the encounter takes place in silence, with a single hand gesture. Despite their determination to demonstrate superiority over the immigrant Sharks, the Jets (both real and in the play) are perfectly willing to actively plagiarize the best of what the Sharks have to offer—that is, their mode of communication. It's a dichotomy that runs throughout the rehearsal process as, time and time again, issues of Deaf or hearing culture impose themselves on the production. This is theater as educational process, and Diane begins to suspect that maintaining this interplay is the best possible reason to continue.

On certain bad days, it becomes the only reason to continue.

Maria

> I remember Steve and I, poor bastards that we were, trying by ourselves at a piano to audition this score for Columbia Records, my record company. They said no, there's nothing in it anybody could sing, too depressing, too many tritones, too many words in the lyrics, too rangy— "Ma-ri-a"—nobody could sing notes like that, impossible. They turned it down.
>
> Leonard Bernstein[1]

Until the final week of rehearsals, Pearlene Jo, the actress chosen to portray Maria, displays an uncanny knack for losing, from one rehearsal to the next, her lines, her cues, and even the most basic elements of her blocking. Despite a winning audition, she demonstrates an almost negligible learning curve through week after slogging week of scene work. Pearlene's fellow actors are generally patient with her fits and starts, her questions, and her nervousness, but, as opening night looms closer, they begin to take out their frustrations on her—and they often do so in ways that completely disrupt Diane's attempts to help her. Shark Michael Nesmith shows particular annoyance at Pearlene's failure to act her way through scenes, and he takes to signing suggestions to her—often violently, with obvious aggression and anger—which leaves Pearlene close to tears more than once. Diane's power to rein in Michael has never been strong, and the fact that he makes his editorial comments in sign language greatly reduces her ability to stop his outbursts. No matter how quickly Diane stamps her foot (a standard method for getting the attention of deaf people) and demands that he stop, she is almost never quick enough to keep Pearlene from both seeing Michael's derision and then responding with tearful recriminations of her own. The situation grows worse and worse as other actors join in with equally snide remarks (thus proving that high school remains high school, no matter what the level of hearing). The low point comes on the Friday before opening night, a rehearsal that leaves even Terri Benz gripping the edges of her piano bench, praying as she does so that Pearlene can get through a single line of Maria's dramatic finale on her own. As both gangs look on in horror—both real and acted—Pearlene clutches Chino's purloined gun and contemplates taking her life. But, with Tony dead on the ground at her feet, Pearlene fumbles one line after another and finally turns to the stage managers (whose assistance is verboten at this point), imploring them for help.

Pearlene is a sophomore in the high school at ISD, a basketball player and substitute track runner. She has a bright smile and her straight brown hair falls to the back of her neck and is forever getting into her face. Although she does not look especially Puerto Rican, she can, when the mood takes her, look surprisingly like Natalie Wood. Her full name is Pearlene Jo Theriot, but she has no contact with her father ("He didn't raise me"), and so insists on going by her first name, not unlike Cher or Madonna, both of whom she admires. She further tweaks her name when using e-mail so that it reads "Pearlene The Riot," or on other messages, "Pearly Jo." When she refers in writing to her fellow ISD students, she identifies them as "the deafies."

Pearlene is a typical American teenager in that she combines a heightened insecurity with a lively streak of vanity. Appearance, however, is not as significant to her as the fact that she is not, and probably cannot be, model thin. Pearlene has no objection to flouncing onto the stage with messy hair, or even in a revealing nightdress, provided it doesn't "make me look fat." (The only moment when the nightdress becomes a source of embarrassment is on the second night of the performances, when Pearlene makes the mistake of wearing polka-dotted underwear instead of indiscernible white.)

Pearlene hates music. As a profoundly deaf person, music, for Pearlene, is unreachable, a coded and mysterious world whose portals remain firmly shut against her. Now she is suddenly being asked to cross a cultural divide of enormous proportions. Even if the message has never been explicit, Pearlene, like many Deaf children hailing from Deaf families, has been socially channeled away from music starting at a very young age. By virtue of the fact that she cannot hear or sing music, music appreciation in itself becomes a foreign language. Her involvement in *West Side Story* demands that she participate in a world that has always been held, both literally and culturally, at bay. She chafes against the sheer number of songs associated with her character and wishes that they would simply go away. Even the rhythms of the songs annoy her, in that she has to match her sign to the beat.

With spoken English in general, interpreted sign moves far too slowly to keep up, but in songs, the opposite may often be true, especially in slow numbers such as "Tonight" and "I Have a Love." Diane experiments with having Pearlene stand at the piano, as Christopher sometimes does, so that she can feel the notes amplified through the wood. She shakes her head: It isn't helping. Next, Diane places Pearlene back-to-back with Dawn, her voicer, and asks Dawn to sing through "Tonight." Again, Pearlene shakes her head. Diane moves the two actors so that they stand face-to-face and has Pearlene place her hand high on Dawn's chest. Pearlene still can't feel the vibrations—until she moves her hand up to Dawn's throat. Dawn then sings each of her songs in turn. She shows Pearlene a copy of the vocal score and teaches her the basics of timing and musical notation. Pearlene shows improvement thereafter, but she continues to tackle the songs too quickly, finishing not just notes or measures before the singers, but sometimes beating them to the end by entire phrases. Christopher eventually discovers that Pearlene does own a hearing aid, but hates using it. He convinces her to wear it for a few rehearsals, with the result that she manages to hear snatches of the music, but not clearly enough to separate the piano from the vocals, or hear the gaps between the words. She has, in the parlance of audiology, sound awareness but not discrimination.

Carrie Moore pitches in, meeting with Pearlene frequently during her regular trips to ISD. They run lines, go over blocking, and talk about motivations. Pearlene tells Carrie that these sessions are boosting her self-confidence, but no amount of self-confidence appears to affect her ability to memorize her lines. Pearlene's lapses are ironic since she is decidedly verbal. For a high schooler, and a deaf high schooler in particular, she is an exceptionally able and avid reader, having recently plowed her way through *Angela's Ashes*, *The Starlite Drive-In*, and Judy Blume's *Summer Sisters*. Her verbal proclivities extend to the initial translation of *West Side Story*'s script, which she works out on her own, then argues her way through a final version with Carrie, word by word and sign by sign. When she becomes stuck on Maria's Spanish phrases (*"Una poca poca"*), Pearlene contacts friends who know the Spanish and has them turn the words into viable English so that she, in turn, can adapt them to ASL. Although a native ASL signer, she "feels she can live in both worlds," meaning she is perfectly at home with Signed English or an amalgam of any sign system that presents itself.

Christopher latches on to Pearlene's love of the written word as a way to coach her through "I Feel Pretty," the song that frustrates Pearlene most. Christopher, who can barely catch the melody himself, insists that she must try to find the spirit of the music and link her character to its happy, buoyant feel.

Pearlene shakes her head in frustration and her hair flies across her face. "Why," she asks, "should I connect with the music when I can't hear the music?"

Christopher hesitates, then takes a risk. "Forget about the music," he tells her. "Use the poetry. Use what the words are telling you."

That clicks. Pearlene abandons her attempts to concentrate on the piano—from most positions on the stage, she can't see Terri's fingers (a potential visual cue)—and she listens, instead, to the text itself, to Stephen Sondheim's lyrics freed as never before from Bernstein's rollicking music. Little by little, Maria's emotions replace Pearlene's frustration; song by song, Maria and Pearlene blend into one.

Diane's own breakthrough in directing Pearlene comes almost too late to be of use. Traditional motivations and various acting tricks and styles have had little effect, but late in the game, while watching Pearlene sign during a scene, Diane has an epiphany. Pearlene, accustomed to relying on physical gestures to communicate her moods, needs strictly physical direction. Diane tests her hypothesis in a bridal shop scene where Maria, positively giddy with anticipation over Tony's impending visit, can hardly sit still. To coax Pearlene into Maria's frame of mind, Diane tells her to behave exactly as she would in her own dorm room, "horsing around" with friends. Pearlene immediately becomes a giggly, smitten schoolgirl. From that moment on, Diane plies the opposite trade from Christopher (who continues to stress poetry) and asks Pearlene to react only with specific physical memories and stances. The dual approach begins to pay off. With spoken lines, Pearlene learns to rely on physical cues, attitudes born of body language and posture; with lyrics, she sinks into the words themselves, their literary quality, their (for her, unheard) poetry.

Maria's Tony makes things at once easier and harder for Pearlene. To the surprise of many students and not a few faculty, it is Ken Roumpos, the actor whom Diane had originally hoped to have as Tony, who steps in to fill the breach. Ken had not expected to be free due to student teaching commitments, a fact he'd made known to Diane in the fall of 1999, and it was his unavailability that led directly to the casting of Scott Corbin, now long gone. Ken is a Mac senior, a Music Education major soon to be married. He's heavy, gifted with a charming smile that fits nicely with his baby face, and he seems tremendously more mature than most of his Mac fellows, a trait which partially accounts for his position as student body president. He sings tenor in the college choir and also performs with a smaller group, including several *West Side Story* cast members, called the MacMurray Singers. On stage, he proves to be the kind of flexible and willing actor any director would wish for. It seems that everything comes easily to him. Pearlene struggles to recall her lines right up to the end, but Ken memorizes his in a matter of a few short weeks. When blocking confuses Pearlene, Ken helps guide her through the motions. They are as different during rehearsals as night and day, with Ken the quick, fluid study, and Pearlene the awkward stepchild, fighting to get something—anything—right.

Ken has one clear advantage over Pearlene: experience. He is twenty-two to Pearlene's fifteen. Pearlene expresses, more than once, her perturbation with having to act the role of a teenager in love when she herself has never had a boyfriend. Over e-mail, she writes to Diane that, "It's hard because I am totally not very romantic. Um, i haven't felt any loss of death yet in my life." The twin hurdles of music and passion conspire against her nightly, and despite her formidable work ethic and obvious willingness to please, one rehearsal after another leaves her close to tears.

Group scenes, however, show her at her best. Freed from the shackles of worrying about romance—and getting romance right—she becomes something of a leader. She encourages her classmates to put their all into each moment on stage. During a mid-March rehearsal, she stamps her foot and demands of the room at large, "Try harder! When are we ever going to get a chance to act with hearing actors again?"

Acting, in and of itself, is important to Pearlene. It carries a certain familial cachet, mostly due to her aunt Terrylene, a pro-

Singing "One Hand, One Heart," Maria and Tony take their vows as Dawn Williams (above, on scaffolding) provides voice interpretation.

fessional actress who is deaf and who, like Pearlene, prefers to drop her last name. Terrylene has been very supportive of Pearlene's *West Side* endeavors, but she lives far away, and the daily reality of Pearlene's situation comes back again and again to Diane, Christopher, and Terri, each with their opinions, their adjustments, their endless and maddening insistence that Pearlene excel.

Dancing completes the triumvirate of Pearlene's difficulties. In staging "I Feel Pretty," Christopher has to avoid almost entirely any legitimate dance steps. Dancing, for Pearlene, is integrally linked to music, and dislike of the former has bred something close to contempt for the latter. "Dance at the Gym" requires her to perform a simplified mambo, which she masters, but not without a struggle. Luckily, no other scene contains explicit directions that Maria herself dance—at least, not until "I Feel Pretty," which opens the second act. Maria, still unaware that Riff and her brother, Bernardo, have been killed, is in a fine, sunny mood; she knows only that Tony has gone to stop the rumble and that she can't wait to see him afterward. While three of her girlfriends look on in wonderment, she flits around the bridal shop, telling all the world that "a committee should be organized to honor me!"

Unfortunately, nothing in the number works. Of the three girlfriends, only Amy Dignan has any hearing to speak of, whereas Jocelyn Cleary and Jeanne Kujawa are profoundly deaf and have at least as much trouble as Pearlene at picking out the timing and feel of the movements. Christopher tinkers with the piece again and again, sometimes taking the rehearsals back to ISD and working on it in Burns Gymnasium on Saturday mornings. But, much as it wants to fly, "I Feel Pretty" simply lumbers. Is this, Diane wonders, the brick wall of deaf musical theater?

Olivia Frome wonders much the same thing, and just as her character, Anita, would likely do, she decides to take matters into

Maria and Rosalia (Jeanne Kujawa) open Act Two in the bridal shop.

her own hands. She begins by demanding that Pearlene accompany her to afternoon and even postrehearsal run-throughs of "A Boy Like That" and other songs; she insists, much to Pearlene's annoyance, that Pearlene needs the extra work. Pearlene drags her feet but eventually accedes to Olivia's demands, and together, they run through the lines and the pacing again and again, inching closer to the timing that Diane and Christopher hope for. After several weeks of private rehearsals, Olivia loses interest, but Pearlene then turns the tables. She senses the progress she's made and she becomes adamant that their practice sessions go on. Olivia huffs and complains but—most days—agrees to continue.

Olivia is not as enamored of *West Side Story* as she was when she began, partly because she and CJ, who were dating when the show began, have since broken up. Much to Olivia's chagrin, CJ plays Bernardo, Anita's lover, so Olivia and CJ must act out a certain minimum intimacy, including what ought to be a smoldering kiss just before "America." Olivia protests initially, and tells Diane to "forget it" regarding the kiss. Diane proves to be equally obstinate and insists that this is what acting is all about. She tells both CJ and Olivia to get over their high school romance and play their parts. Olivia fusses for weeks and CJ, reserved already, becomes positively remote. Olivia keeps her spirits up by focusing on her goal of returning next year to her local (hearing) school, Tinley Park, where she wants to get back into cheerleading, an activity she's been kicked out of at ISD. Olivia's sudden exit from cheerleading nearly cost her any part in *West Side Story*. The team's coach is Cara Hammond, and Cara did not appreciate Olivia's lip or attitude. Cara also serves as Olivia's speech therapist, and she works with Olivia almost daily to improve her pronunciation of related sounds like *s* and *th*. As a result of the cheerleading fiasco, Cara suggested to Diane in late January that it might be wise to let Olivia go immediately, before she can make a real nuisance of herself. Diane arranged a special meeting with

Olivia, took her emotional pulse, and exacted a promise from Olivia that she would stick out *West Side Story*, come hell or high water.

Now, plagued by her breakup with CJ and Pearlene's endless desire to rehearse, Olivia wonders if brimstone and floods might be preferable to staying on. Quitting sounds increasingly tempting, especially with Diane and the production team riding her about getting her lines signed in legible ASL. Olivia pleads that it would be easier to use Signed English, but again, Diane will not be moved. "You need to use ASL because you're playing a member of a Deaf community," she says, choosing not to broach her suspicion that the Puerto Rican Deaf aren't likely to use anything remotely similar to ASL. After her one semester of ASL with Bob Dramin, Diane is all too aware that she is even further from mastering the language than is Olivia, but this only makes her all the more aware that she has a significant problem on her hands when she spots Olivia mixing the signs for *better* in the line, "You better be home in fifteen minutes." Olivia knows only the qualitative version of the word, indicating that Maria will be better—healthier, improved in some way—if she gets home quickly. Diane concludes, correctly, that if a neophyte like herself can spot errors in Olivia's signing, then Deaf audiences will poke holes in her language from beginning to end. BETTER becomes only the first of many signs the production team forces Olivia to change, and each change becomes a fresh battle, a little extra ammunition pushing Olivia to pack her things and walk.

Unbeknownst to the production team, Pearlene almost packed her bags before auditions even began. She told herself that she didn't have the time, that she didn't like music anyway. She even convinced herself, briefly, that students with better hearing—namely Olivia—would garner all the parts. Now that rehearsals have begun, however, she never gives up—on herself, on Olivia, or anyone else. Midway through the rehearsal process, Jocelyn suddenly refuses to go back onto the stage for another run-through of "I Feel Pretty." Christopher, despite his entreaties, cannot get Jocelyn to budge. Diane has already given up on Jocelyn for the evening, and has begun to consider firing her. Pearlene suddenly takes charge, demanding through a sheet of angry tears that Jocelyn get on her feet and work the scene— for her sake, for Christopher's sake, for the sake of the play itself. To Christopher's amazement, Jocelyn relents, and the rehearsal continues. Christopher's respect for his young star grows from that night on, and he begins to describe her as "brave" and "holding onto my hand while I hold her over a cliff." She still claims to understand nothing of love, music, or dance—yet she continues to fight for all three.

America

The Deaf community is a concept, not a place, and those who cannot hear choose whether or not they want to belong.

Nanci A. Scheetz
Orientation to Deafness[1]

Mac and ISD have embarked on *West Side Story* during what promises to be a key election year, yet neither the Republican nor Democratic camps, led by George W. Bush and Al Gore, respectively, show the least interest in courting the votes of the Deaf community. This is business as usual insofar as political strategists concentrate almost exclusively on racial, religious, or regional groupings; they have no interest in ferreting out the many smaller, statistically useless groups (from a vote-getting perspective) that pepper the nation. Common (hearing) consensus holds that deaf citizens are among those groups, ostracized less by design than by noninclusion. Nobody seeks their input and, while several important pieces of legislation have slowly congealed into a recognizable and usable body of laws, it seems clear that, on a day-to-day basis, lawmakers, like most Americans, don't think about deafness any more than they think about Mars.

In any event, the Deaf community is hardly cohesive enough to form an ongoing voting bloc. Rough estimates suggest that some two million Americans are unable to hear spoken language, and approximately sixteen million Americans have some degree of hearing loss. This second number includes those who lose their hearing, to even a small degree, through natural aging processes or other environmental factors. It makes no distinction between those who are deaf from birth and those who lose their hearing, by accident or genetic predisposition, during life. For example, who has not encountered a relative or acquaintance who refuses to accept or acknowledge his or her obvious and increasing hearing loss. Given such varied definitions, it is a wonder that deaf people can be spoken of as constituting a group at all, and yet, a healthy Deaf community thrives, not merely in the United States, but worldwide. If any one thing links this community together, it would have to be a basic and tangible pride in deafness itself.

Pride, however, has not always translated into either clout or unity. The Americans with Disabilities Act (ADA) represents very recent legislation, signed into law on July 26, 1990. With ADA on the books, all businesses, public offices, and public spaces must be prepared to communicate effectively with deaf citizens. Making effective communication a reality has proven to be a painstakingly slow process, because it presents very different problems from the law's more physical ramifications, such as increasing the aisle widths in public places to accommodate wheelchairs. The latter can be effected with hardware and updated building codes—physical changes designed to produce quick physical results. It is another matter entirely to educate a nation on the linguistic and other needs of deaf citizenry. Most face-to-face deaf and hearing interactions still boil down to pointing and note writing. The advent of technological breakthroughs such as real-time captioning, operator-assisted relay calls, TTYs, and e-mail have paved over some obvious rough spots, but none of these can alleviate the basic fact that many deaf people have limited or nonexistent oral skills, and most hearing people know little to nothing about any form of sign language, much less the demanding syntax of ASL.

If all signers in the United States were lumped together and assumed to use ASL, one could make a quick case that ASL is the fourth most popular language used in the country today. In reality, this is something of a pipe dream. More realistic estimates suggest that somewhere between 300,000 and 500,000 people actually employ ASL as their first language. Nevertheless, it is undeniably clear that ASL, both as a linguistic medium and a symbol of ongoing creative expression, is a source of tremendous self-esteem for those within the Deaf community.

Deaf people tend to see Deaf culture as vibrant and worthy of both attention and study, yet such attention has been fleeting at best from a society dominated and saturated by a very auditory media. Some events seen as key to Deaf culture remain virtually unknown to the hearing community. For example, books (not to mention web pages) written by Deaf individuals repeatedly cite the importance of the 1988 ouster of Gallaudet University's last hearing president. Gallaudet came into being in 1864, founded by Edward Miner Gallaudet and chartered by the United States Congress as the National Deaf-Mute College, based on terminology in vogue at the time. Although many hearing people never learn of Gallaudet's existence, it is renowned in the international Deaf community as the only liberal arts university designed specifically for Deaf people. Members of the Deaf community view the 1988 protests as a political watershed, a triumph akin to, if somewhat smaller in scale than, the Civil Rights marches of the 1960s. Unfortunately, the hearing world has little or no memory of the Gallaudet revolt one way or the other. It has passed by the national consciousness as just another drop in the infinite bucket of late-breaking news.

Like it or not, it seems that ASL and the Deaf community will remain isolated—sometimes cheerfully, sometimes not—from much of mainstream America, at least for the immediate future. ASL is after all a "foreign" language, one not often taught in high schools geared to hearing students. Hearing students are beguiled instead by more traditional and widely available choices like French, Spanish, or Chinese. Although a number of colleges and universities offer ASL classes, for many potential students, it's an encounter that comes too late (as it probably has for this author), with the result that ASL signers form a linguistic elite, fluent in a language that has little application outside of the Deaf community. Regardless of its beauty, efficiency, or inherent cultural value, ASL is a language with decided limitations as long as it exists only in pockets, pockets that exist within the strictures of a generally hearing world.

Those pockets seem all the smaller when one considers that ASL is not, by any means, a worldwide standard. Put another way, the "American" in American Sign Language is not there for show. While the ease of international travel and the United States' cultural dominance has made ASL a second (signed) language for many deaf people across the globe, it is still true that members of the Deaf communities in, say, Mexico and England would find it exceedingly difficult to understand their Deaf peers in the United States, and vice versa. Signs have evolved locally, sometimes regionally, in many places and many nations.

A real case has been made to assign ASL the status of a complete language system. Authors of books on the subject go to great (and sometimes slightly hysterical) lengths to impress upon the reader just how different English and ASL actually are. The arguments are persuasive. ASL contains clear linguistic elements such as tense indicators, classifiers, verbs that incorporate direction, and the repetition of signs to hone specific meanings.[2] Nor are the hands the only tools employed by ASL; a listener must also attend to the myriad (often specific) facial expressions of the signer and even to posture. Certain signs encompass what would, in English, entail more than one word or concept, as in "I give you a present." In ASL, "I give you" is a single sign, I-GIVE-YOU. Word order may also change relative to English, such that "I threw the girl the ball," if signed in ASL and then translated one sign at a time (rather than as a concept or complete statement) into English, would be *Girl there finish me ball throw*. Sometimes the changes go beyond mere alterations in the sequence of words. To ask the English question, "Have you ever been to California?" will come back in ASL as TOUCH FINISH CALIFORNIA YOU with the signer's eyebrows raised. When ASL is written as English, it becomes obvious that certain connecting words, such as definite and indirect articles, are missing. Because ASL does not include a past tense marker for verbs, many sentences open with a reference to time so that anyone viewing the message will understand whether the event described occurred in the past, is occurring in the present, or will occur in the future. All in all, a linguistic basket quite separate from English—or, to misquote Edmund Spenser, "a well of English most beautifully defiled."

If ASL's development can be traced back to a single moment in time, the year would be 1817, when Laurent Clerc, himself deaf, and Thomas Hopkins Gallaudet (Edward's father) founded the United States' first permanent school for the deaf in Hartford, Connecticut. Gallaudet and Clerc met in Paris, where they had both studied a French system of sign language now known as Methodical Signs, created years before by Abbé de L'Epee. Clerc was also fluent in Old French Sign Language, which was the basis of Methodical Sign. With the creation of their new school, christened the Connecticut Asylum for the Education and Instruction of Deaf and Dumb Persons, Clerc and Gallaudet set about codifying this language into an acceptable tool for American children and signers in general. The result: ASL, which still contains remnants of its French progenitor. Some estimates suggest that fully 60 percent of ASL signs are influenced by Old French Sign Language, if not in concept, then in origin.[3] The remaining 40 percent come from the sign languages in use in parts of the United States before 1817 and interactions with deaf people from other countries, much like any other language system. The little Hartford school also has prospered and remains in operation; it is now called the American School for the Deaf.

In 1880, an international movement gained currency that declared oralism (the use of speech and speechreading) to be preferable to sign language, and hearing teachers, intent on demonstrating the wonders of speechreading, quickly took over. It was not until well into the 1960s that sign language reemerged as an alternative method of communication in schools. The choice of communication method remains a controversial topic even today, and the use of speech by a deaf or hard of hearing person can become either an unwitting or a willful political act. Like deafness in general, the term *oralism* can be difficult to pin down. Referring to a person as oral might indicate someone who chooses to use his or her voice with hearing people—Christopher Smith, for example.

The oral versus manual debate has been described by Beryl Lieff Benderly, author of *Dancing Without Music: Deafness in America*, as "a holy war."[4] It's an issue that has sunk its considerable teeth into the broader educational realm—a realm dominated by hearing people. Hearing people, unfortunately (but predictably), understand deafness best by analogy or as an absence of sound perception. The leap to perceiving deafness as the progenitor of a legitimate Deaf culture remains uncommon at best. As described by Douglas C. Baynton, "The deaf community finds itself endlessly on the defensive, trying to find hearing educators willing to listen to them. . . . Given the wealth of experience that deaf adults have to draw on, it is a constant source of puzzlement and pain how little their advice is heeded."[5]

Baynton argues that the heart of the arguments over oral vs. manual communication lay in what the hearing world perceived as natural. Consider this admonition from Alexander Graham Bell, speaking at the Convention of Articulation Teachers of the Deaf in 1884:

> We should try ourselves to forget that they are deaf. We should
> teach them to forget that they are deaf. We should speak to them
> naturally and with the same voice that we speak to other people,
> and avoid unnatural movements of the mouth or anything that
> would mark them as different from others.[6]

For a devout oralist like Bell, *natural* (as Baynton expertly
demonstrates) had come to mean "normal," and any deaf behav-
ior or decision regarding the education of deaf individuals would
be measured against the normalcy of the hearing populace.
Vocalized speech was, according to the oralists, the natural way
for civilized humans to communicate. Anything else would be
downright barbaric, a mockery of civilization and progress.

Turn-of-the-century manualists used the word *natural* differently, aiming away from "normal" (essentially a statistical referent) and toward an alignment with nature itself, stressing that
gestures and body language were then and always had been perfectly natural outgrowths of the human form—and thus, of
nature in the broadest sense. Sign language, according to the
manualists, was merely an advancement of the sort of pantomime
that all people engage in daily, a pantomime that includes smiling, pointing, shrugging, and so on. To separate sign language
from other physical movements, to place it on one side of a divid-
ing line was, to manualists, fundamentally misguided (read
unnatural) and clearly an egregious error.[7]

Oralists were consistently resisted by the Deaf community, at
least in part because oralism implied assimilation into hearing culture. Manualists (who were also not to be entirely trusted, given
that they, too, were a hearing group) generally won the support of
deaf people because, as Baynton puts it, "manualism allowed the
possibility of alternative constructions of deafness by deaf people
themselves . . . they could resist the meanings that hearing people
attached to deafness, adopt them . . . or create their own."[8]

In recent times, manualism is again ascendant, and the tar-
nished image of sign language has now been polished to a healthy

shine. Educators fluent in ASL are not so scarce as they once were, but even today, those who know ASL may side with the majority view that education should bring deaf students as close as possible to full-fledged English-and-ASL bilingualism. This shifts the focus away from mastery of ASL, a skill that some schools tacitly assume can still be learned and practiced at home or amongst peers and mentors within the Deaf community. Instead, the academic curriculum is taught through various sign systems structured around an English base. Among these systems are Manually Coded English (MCE) and systems such as Signed English, Seeing Essential English (SEE I), Signing Exact English (SEE II), and Total Communication (TC).

TC employs speech, the use of residual hearing, signing, and fingerspelling and is used in many schools. Like the other systems mentioned above, TC was developed to help deaf children learn to read and write English. Using slightly different strategies, these systems advocate using ASL signs in English word order. Some add markers (invented signs or fingerspelling) to make visible those elements of English that are not signed in ASL. For example, verb endings such as -ed and -ing do not have signs in ASL, so invented signs are added at the end of an otherwise accurate ASL sign in Signed English and SEE II.

Fingerspelling, formally known as dactylology (but sometimes called the Great Invention), introduced a single handshape for each correspondent letter of the alphabet. Thus, for twenty-six letters, there are twenty-six shapes. Because fingerspelling is a literal representation of spoken language, it has no syntax, no independent means of expressing thought or ideas. It delivers its information with the coolness of Morse or binary code. On the plus side, it is very—sometimes harshly—clear. When two signers fail to understand one another, fingerspelling provides a concrete, unambiguous solution.

Whatever one may think of oralism as a method of communication, it is not without its dramatic uses onstage. Late in the second act of *West Side Story*, Anita risks entering Doc's drugstore to deliver a message to Tony. She is soon set upon by the Jets, who in a flash of sudden violence, come close to raping her. (In the ongoing debate over the play's stereotyping of Puerto Ricans, nothing much seems to be made of the fact that it is the Jets—the friendly, chummy Jets—who come closest to committing a rape.) Only Doc's sudden arrival halts the mayhem. In the Mac/ISD production, this scene presents Diane with a serious dilemma, in that here, for the first and only time, the actress playing Anybodys and voicing Anita has lines for both characters in the same scene. Because Meredith cannot be both Anybodys and the voice of Anita simultaneously, Diane falls back on the fact that Olivia (as Anita) has exceptionally good speaking skills. When pressed too hard by the Jets, Olivia suddenly screams at them and, in perfect English, delivers her line—"Listen you!"—vocally. The Jets, stunned to discover that one of the "Puerto Rican spics" can talk, stand back and give her space. It turns out to be one of the most effective moments in the play, one that audience members specifically remember and comment upon when filling out post-show surveys.

Christopher himself would prefer to avoid what he sees as the limiting terms of the communication debate. He would rather not be put in boxes and labeled—but, as he says with a resigned shrug, it's something he has to live with. When pressed, he places himself firmly in the middle, which makes perfect sense given his choice of career. He will, as a performing artist, be in constant contact with the hearing world. Adopting an isolationist stance would be difficult, if not impossible. In any event, deafness is hardly the only cross he has to bear. As a black man and a dancer, he has more than enough boxes to go around without adding levels of deafness to the till.

The Jets harass Anita (Olivia Frome, center with belt scarf) as she attempts to deliver Maria's message to Tony. The Jets from left are A-Rab (Prentice Southwell), Baby John (Bryce Hoffman), Diesel (Dane Vincent), Action (Richard Atkins), and Anybodys (Meredith Blair).

If Mac has a national reputation in any department, it lies square-ly on the shoulders of Deaf Education. Its heavily accredited teacher education program is the largest and oldest in Illinois and it now boasts an interpreter training program headed up by Bob Dramin. Graduates through the year 2000 receive either a B.S. or, if they fulfill a language requirement with French or Spanish, a B.A. Starting with the graduating class of 2001, ASL will also count toward a B.A. Graduates may then apply for an Illinois teaching certificate (kindergarten through twelfth grade), focus-ing on work with deaf and hard-of-hearing students. Incoming students certainly find ISD's proximity a strong draw, and the possibility of rooming at ISD provides the kind of immersion in Deaf culture that most colleges can only provide through text-books and description. In class, Deaf Ed majors proceed through a maze of required courses such as Manually Coded English,

Instructional Technology, and the ever-popular English elective. The only way to complete the major in the traditional four collegiate years is to begin freshman year, first semester.

Some seventy Mac students (some of whom are themselves deaf), currently identify Deaf Education as their major, making it the most popular discipline on campus. Virtually all the Deaf Edders are women. At last count, only two male students were enrolled in the program. A disproportionate amount of Mac's academic talent finds its way here; with fifteen students receiving honors at the end of the 1999–2000 academic year, seven hail from Deaf Ed. Students view the atmosphere within the department as competitive, sometimes to a fault. Faculty occasionally wonder whether the better student signers wind up driving others from the program, either through peer pressure or more direct confrontation. Perhaps the weeding out is natural, since Deaf Ed, unlike most other majors, isn't likely to automatically vanish beyond the threshold of the classroom. Deaf Ed isn't simply a program designed to teach a method of communication, and it isn't merely the exposition of a pedagogical philosophy. It's a lifestyle, complete unto itself. For Deaf Ed majors, mere competency is simply unacceptable—only mastery counts.

The fractures within the major bleed out into the MacMurray Educational Association for the Deaf (MEAD), a student-run club designed to provide an extracurricular deaf-oriented learning experience. MEAD has undergone several name changes in the last few years, beginning as Silent Majority, then switching, after objections, to Deaf Adventure. The tendentious politics of Deaf community directly affect MEAD, sometimes to the detriment of membership. In the spring of 1999, attendance had fallen to just ten to fifteen students per meeting. However, the club shows no sign of vanishing. It continues to organize social and community activities, and sponsors a "voices off" bowling night with ISD's high school. Guest speakers remain a popular draw, and attendance, despite the fact that some students still view the entire group as cagey, clique-ridden, and even downright bitchy, has been on the rise.

Nor are there any signs of the department itself folding, despite many swings and staff changes. While admitting that Mac generally fields an excellent program, ISD's Steve Tavender notes that it has not always been as solid as it is today. He is still prepared for a certain number of subpar student teachers arriving on his campus through Deaf Ed, but he remembers times—not so long ago—when the numbers of unacceptable, even failing, student teachers was unbearably high. "They just weren't turning out a very good product," he recalls, referring to Mac.

Recent recruits have been much better, and the relationship between the two schools is again strong. Still, when student teachers don't meet ISD's standards, Steve cuts them, culling the wheat from the chaff as quickly and painlessly as he can. He insists, however, that deafness and Deaf issues typically aren't the problem. It is the consensus of ISD's staff that the student teachers who are asked to leave ISD's classrooms would have failed in any classroom environment.

ISD, meanwhile, has itself fallen on hard times. A residential school, it boasted a peak enrollment of around six hundred students. Today, barely half that attend, and many of these do so not because of profound deafness, but because their neighborhood schools cannot accommodate them or they have difficult home lives. The reasons for the decline are legion, but the major factor is certainly Public Law 94-142, also known as the Education for All Handicapped Children Act of 1975, now called the Individuals with Disabilities Education Act (IDEA). This law states that deaf children are entitled to an education in their local school districts. On the surface, this seems perfectly benign, even helpful, but it raises the same wasp's nest of problems currently experienced by California and other states engaged in the hearing world's own version of the bilingualism debate.

The implication—not so deeply buried—is that integration can and should be the dominant goal for any given deaf child, and that it is up to the broader (hearing) educational system to help them achieve this integration. Many members of the Deaf community charge that IDEA undermines a deaf child's proper development by robbing them of the chance to immerse themselves in Deaf culture, surrounded, as they would be at ISD or similar residential schools, with other deaf (and Deaf) persons. A more militant interpretation (and militant, in the Jacksonville area, is referred to as "Deaf Deaf") would be that the law actually steals children in that it prevents them from finding their real community. This view concludes that the law is effectively destroying the Deaf community from within, through simple attrition.

Even when residential schools are cheap or free, many parents want to keep their child close to home. IDEA gives them the legal precedent to do so because it forces local schools to accept deaf students and adapt to their needs as best they can. The concept has had several labels (e.g., mainstreaming, inclusion), and its merits, like bilingualism, continue to be debated daily. Whether by accident or design, mainstreaming has much in common with the goals of nineteenth-century oralists. Consider the words of educator Emma Garrett, who in 1893 saw fit to write that the "ideal education for a deaf child was that he should never see another deaf child."[9] With mainstreaming, this is not only entirely possible, it is commonplace. A deaf student attending public (hearing) schools may well be the only deaf child in his or her classroom—or in the school at large. Critics charge that such children will be disenfranchised rather than included, and they argue that a deaf child will never fit fully into a hearing world. The critics' case is easy to put in concrete terms: imagine being the only child with a personal interpreter present for all classes—but not necessarily between classes or at lunch, when so much key socializing (and socialization) takes place. A better recipe for ostracization would be difficult to conjure.

Pro or con, the mainstreaming of deaf children is a debate defined at least in part by its necessarily ongoing nature. Hearing people who emigrate to a new country may eventually learn that area's native tongue (as the Sharks have learned English in *West Side Story*), but deaf children will always be deaf and will always require special services. With or without political recognition, this is one minority bloc that stands little chance of being assimilated.

Cool/Tonight

Hail to MacMurray, the pride of us all

Hail to our alma mater, may her standards never fall

Hail to MacMurray, we pledge our loyalty

Knowledge, Faith and Service shall our ensign ever be.

Wisdom gained through college illuminates the way

How to meet with reverence the duties of each day

Thus our code is molded to lead a loyal clan

Wisdom, Duty, Reverence shall be our goal and plan.

"Hail to MacMurray," the College Song
Kane, Smith, and Wolff

Feburary 2000. The Mac theater space cannot contain its own rehearsals. Actors spill out the doors, flood the hallways, and seep into lecture halls and classrooms. Two and sometimes three separate groups rehearse all at once, with Diane bouncing between them as best she can. Terri runs through the vocal numbers while Christopher leads his troops through the dance and fight routines again . . . and again . . . and again. Scenes with neither music nor dancing are Diane's particular province. Whenever she can, she takes actors away from the main space and works with them in small groups, forcing intimacies between people who would normally avoid any such thing.

Warming up before rehearsal.

For Ken Roumpos and Pearlene Jo (Tony and Maria), the process is painless enough. Diane puts Ken and Pearlene in an empty classroom and hands each of the two, in turn, a piece of paper with a single word written on it, such as "Happy," "Sick," or "Annoyed." If Pearlene has the word, then it is Ken's job to guess her mimed word and write it down. The pair employs gestures, touch, and bad overacting to get messages across, not unlike a game of charades. Becky Cline, a history teacher at ISD, helps explain the rules, but does no interpreting once the guessing begins. After a few rounds, Diane ups the ante and hands out slips with declarative sentences such as "I am sad" or "You are cute." Dawn Williams joins the games as Pearlene's voice, and she races against both Ken and Pearlene to write the correct answer. Having mastered this, they try for translations of more conceptual phrases such as "Where are you from?" and "How old are you?" These take longer, but all three actors prove to be perceptive mind readers. Diane proceeds to a more difficult variation, where the same basic rules apply but contact is forbidden, and the participants must take up positions on opposite ends of the classroom. Diane wishes to mimic the conditions of the scene where Tony and Maria first meet but remain separated by a vast distance (actually about four feet in the final staging), a distance comprised not only of space but of habit and culture.

At the end of the gaming, Diane asks Pearlene to describe to Ken whatever it is that he absolutely has to know about her in order for them to work together effectively. Pearlene jumps right to her feet and announces, "Never touch my tummy!" Then, as if searching for a more mature, collegiate confession, Pearlene informs Ken that she comes from a multigenerational Deaf family, that she herself represents the sixth deaf generation. (It is an ongoing shock to Pearlene's entire clan that her two sisters are both hearing.) She takes it upon herself to teach Ken a few important ASL signs that will help them communicate, both as people and as actors. The first of these is HI-HOW-ARE-YOU. Pearlene finds Ken to be a reasonable student, quick enough at sign to keep her from getting frustrated. She notes that she has taught many of her hearing friends how to sign and that the only hearing people who make her mad are the ones who "aren't creative or don't try." Pearlene, however, continues to prove a difficult study in the romance department. Believing herself to be in love with Ken (as Tony or anyone else) is a hurdle that literally makes her squirm. Even Ken's rapid progress with the limited signing he's expected to master does little to raise Pearlene's decidedly cool temperature.

The actors playing the Sharks and Jets, enemies on stage, have to be exceptionally trusting in reality. Two full-scale fights, the first in the prologue, the second during the rumble, leave ample room for all-too-real physical damage. At the outset, neither side is ready for either choreography or stage combat techniques; Diane and Christopher begin instead with acting games, not unlike those employed by many college campuses during orientation week. Christopher designs the opening game only to wonder if it might be too invasive, too accidentally intimate, at least for the hearing actors, who are not as used to touch and physical contact as are many of the deaf students. To further complicate matters, the deaf actors are all minors, and the game he has in mind tends to break personal space in surprising ways. Diane reassures him, saying that everything is supervised and he should go ahead.

Christopher proceeds to move the entire group into a circle. With everyone in place, he asks the cast to join hands and then memorize, visually, the person on their left. After thirty seconds, Christopher asks them to look to their right and memorize that person as well. Then he tells everyone to close their eyes, drop hands, and walk slowly away from the circle. Once everyone has become hopelessly randomized, they will have to locate their neighbors by touch and find their way back to the circle—in the same order they started in. The group giggles, anticipating disaster, but they keep their eyes shut, put up their hands to ward off contact, and shuffle away to the four corners of the stage. CJ finds his left-hand partner, Meredith, by accidentally plucking at her eyebrow; she lets out a squawk of protest, and CJ, who wears his hearing aid to rehearsals, realizes he's found the person he's after. CJ's hat gives him away to his right-hand partner, and the circle re-forms in remarkable time.

Another game, line-reading tag, enjoys only limited success. The object is simple: the actors in a given scene literally play tag while reciting their lines. When applied to the Jets, none of them have their lines memorized, which leaves stage manager Carrie Moore reading each line for a Jet to echo. The energy level in the scene rises immediately, but in attempting the same exercise with the deaf actors, Diane gets the opposite result. Unlike the hearing Jets, the Sharks have to stop and watch Carrie to get a line reading, and every time they do, the tag game grinds to a halt.

After a similarly dysfunctional first try at "Dance at the Gym," Diane assembles all her actors for the start of the next rehearsal and has them let off steam by explaining, to each other, not to her, why communication has been so difficult. The actors collapse into a malformed circle and begin complaining to each other—until Joey Gillis (Chino) jumps into the ring of bickering actors and demonstrates a series of gestures that he feels might work for both sides. Joey tells everyone he comes from a hearing family, so he's used to fighting to make himself understood—and he makes it clear that he expects his suggestions to become the local law of the land. In a less-accomplished performance, Joey might have seriously impaired his standing with the group, but he dictates his new, personalized communication system with such dramatic, cornball flair that he has the entire cast and crew, Diane included, laughing. Most of what he comes up with (nudges, show-specific signs, cues for deaf and hearing actors to get each other's attention without interrupting scenes, etc.) becomes unnecessary once the cast memorizes its lines and steps, but at this critical starting point, Joey gives the cast a significant boost. Diane is pleased that he stepped forward, and that her decompression tactic worked. She wonders how many more bitch sessions will be required and whether Joey will have the maturity and verve to lead more in the future.

In early 1999, during a meeting with Cara Hammond and others, Carrie Moore quietly passed Diane a note on a torn-off piece of yellow legal paper. At the top, she wrote, "Are we having an interpreter during the actual rehearsal process?"

Diane wrote back, "Do you think we should?" and Carrie, after a moment's consideration, shook her head no. As the meeting's conversation swirled around them, Diane added another line to the bottom of the sheet: "I don't think so either."

One person who understands just how wrong they are is ISD's Becky Cline. Becky, who is familiar on a first-name basis with virtually all of the ISD students, attends the November auditions and tries to warn Diane, Terri, and Christopher what they're letting themselves in for. Crowd control. Constant interpreting. Potential chaos. The dances, she says, will be impossible to coordinate without an active and qualified interpreter present. Diane doesn't disagree—not after seeing how essential Becky and Carrie are at the auditions—but she has never had the budget for a full-time rehearsal interpreter. Becky muses that she might be able to get special funding from ISD, and Diane agrees to look into reallocating some of her own funds. Becky's presence, however, turns out to be a somewhat mixed blessing. The ISD contingent seems mildly afraid of her, and tends to respond more quickly to her than they do to Carrie, Christopher, or most of the dorm parents. Becky is a fine, expressive interpreter, but Diane catches her, more than once, adding to or modifying her instructions to the actors. Becky brushes off Diane's requests that she not elaborate or provide extra information; Becky makes it clear that she knows best how to reach "these kids" and assures Diane that it will all work out in the wash.

On balance, Becky proves to be a strong asset to the production, and her assistance makes it abundantly clear that large-scale rehearsals could never have proceeded without an interpreter present. Indeed, looking back at the note from Carrie some weeks after the production, Diane just shakes her head. "Wow," she murmurs. "What were we thinking?"

It's a thought echoed by choral director Melanie Jacobson during a preproduction phone call in early February 2000. As the show's official vocal coach, she sees endless pitfalls ahead, especially in regard to the music. After discussing the needs of young voices and the potential abuse and damage that overused vocal chords can suffer, she finally says, "You know, you guys really don't know what you're getting yourselves into."

"Of course," Diane responds. "But, Melanie, if we *really* understood what we were doing, we wouldn't even try. Isn't that part of the point?"

As if Christopher doesn't already have enough on his plate, *West Side Story* (and the number "America," in particular) forces him to come to grips with a subtle musical trick known as hemiola. *The Harvard Concise Dictionary of Music and Musicians* explains it this way: "In terms of rhythm, it refers to the use of three notes of equal value in the time normally occupied by two notes of equal value."[1] *Merriam-Webster's Collegiate Dictionary* tries it as "a musical rhythmic alternation in which six equal notes may be heard as two groups of three or three groups of two."[2] Essentially, the beat relies on a ratio of 3:2, where the first measure is felt in three, the very next in two, the third in three again, and so on. The time signature remains unchanged throughout. Thus, in six-eight time, you have a measure of six eighth notes followed by a measure of three quarter notes. Dancers, who always prefer to work in counts of eight, typically impose their steps on major beats, such that, in four-four time, a single set of eight counts takes up two full measures, as in:

one	two	three	four	/	one	two	three	four
one	two	three	four	/	five	six	seven	eight

In six-eight time, a dancer's eight count requires four full measures to reach its conclusion, and the main beat hits only once per every three counts, as in the following two measures:

one two three *four* five six *one* two three *four* five six
one   two   three   four

It is also common to feel the beat not merely on one and four, but also on one, three and five. This is precisely what occurs in "America," and the added wrinkle of one, three, and five is hemiola; after its inclusion, a dancer's eight count becomes very difficult indeed. Written in six-eight, the main beat remains on one and four only for the first measure; after that, it becomes paired, as in:

one two three *four* five six *one*-two *three*-four *five*-six
"I like to be in A- mer- i- ca"

Christopher listens over and over again to Terri's explanation of hemiola, but nothing sinks in; neither Carrie nor Becky nor anyone else can discover a translation that works.

 Frustrated, Terri spots Jay Peterson in the halls before rehearsal and demands of her former teacher, "All right, Dr. Peterson, answer me this. How do you teach hemiola to a deaf man?" Jay blinks, considers for a moment, and replies that no one has ever asked him that question before. He walks away without offering an answer.

 Terri's solution is to group sequences into either standard six-eight or the hemiola variation of one-two, three-four, five-six, and to tell Christopher how many of each he has to work with, and in what sequence. "You have six of these to work with," she tells him, or, "Try another four sets like that." Christopher puts his hand on the piano, feels the beat, and nods. "O-kay," he says, and sets to work.

 Luckily, thanks in part to Olivia, whose hearing remains as sharp as ever, the dancers in "America" pick up the concept quickly, and Christopher learns it from watching them. The more he sees, the more he revises. Although "The Prologue" and "Dance at the Gym" take longer for the actors to master, no scene requires more time for Christopher than does "America." It is his personal bugbear, a monument to the difficulties of translating even numerical concepts when dancing your way through a brace or more of foreign languages.

Bernstein's surprising opening music typifies one concept that may well defy translation into the deaf world. The Western musical scale contains within it certain harmonic gaps and difficult intervals, and Bernstein delights in testing one of these, the *diabolus in musica* (literally, the devil in the music) during *West Side Story*. It's a fine example of using music to create—and later resolve—dramatic tension, but it is not a tool that the deaf audiences or performers can use to key into the nature of the show. Hearing listeners, however, cannot help but be jarred. Also known as a tritone, the *diabolus in musica* refers to an augmented fourth, the interval between the fourth and fifth steps in a diatonic major scale. Most harmonies rely on the first, fourth, or fifth steps, these being the strongest intervals available, and attempts to sing the half step between the fourth and fifth are made at the singer's peril since the note produced will create a dissonance with any other note played in that scale. Bernstein uses this dissonance to start the show, first from A to D-sharp then from D to G-sharp. These off-putting intervals are, in fact, the first notes heard. Terri, still convinced that Bernstein was a musical sadist, concedes that nevertheless "he was a genius at getting our attention." Sadly, it is not a genius that translates for Christopher or his choreography. He manages to catch the spirit of "The Prologue" regardless, but not from Bernstein's use of tritones. The *diabolus in musica* is one devil that Christopher, most likely, need never worry about.

One Hand, One Heart

"I thought Diane was about out of her mind, and I had faith, but . . ."

Jennifer Harris

In a vintage *Star Trek* episode, Captain Kirk attempts to beam back aboard the *Enterprise* during one of the show's ubiquitous ion storms and gets split into two Kirks. One half of him materializes as a soulful conscience, the other as a vibrant, aggressive leader. The remainder of the episode charts this Tale of Two Kirks to its logical conclusion, the reunification of the useless two into a single champion breed.

Mac's *West Side Story* engenders that same split without the benefit or even hope of such a reunification. From the beginning, each main character has a doppelgänger either voicing or signing the lines of the actor "officially" playing the part. Having made the decision to cast the ISD contingent as the Sharks, Diane has ensured that their doubles will all have to speak. Actors playing the Jets and various adult figures will thus have interpreters capable of signing the lines for a deaf audience.

Conceptually, none of this presents a particular problem, because the needs of the story and the needs of the audience will both be served. In practical terms, the dilemmas seem, at times, to be unending. Perhaps most alarmingly, the necessary doubling of roles swells the cast considerably. Mac's *West Side Story* never has a single Maria; it always has two, right from the start. Likewise, it has two Tonys (eventually), two Anitas, two Riffs, and so on. To confuse matters even further, not a single interpreter or voicer handles just one part or person; through a shortage of skilled or willing bodies, these performers must all adjust to one of the actor's age-old (if sometimes cherished) problems, that of doubling up and tackling more than one role.

Certain characters, however, demand near exclusivity. Maria and Tony, in particular, have such large roles that giving their doubles anything extra to do risks not only confusing the cast but the audience, as well. In the end, Tony's interpreter, Phil Fiorini, comes the closest of any "non-actor" to assuming only one role. Aside from a brief appearance as a mirror during "I Feel Pretty," he does nothing onstage other than shadow for Tony. Dawn Williams's job, centered on her duties as Maria's speaking and singing voice, is much more varied. She also portrays Graziella, one of the Jet's girlfriends. Graziella has only a few spoken lines, but she appears in several scenes, notably "Dance at the Gym." This proves to be a difficult feat, for Dawn begins the scene as a Jet girl, dancing with her Jet boyfriend until, quite suddenly, she has to revert, like Cinderella at midnight, to the voice of Maria for Maria's crucial first meeting with Tony. The blocking alone turns out to be a nightmare; the stage is already at its most crowded, and, worse, it is split down the middle into two very separate camps. The Jets occupy stage right, the Sharks stage left. Dawn, as Graziella, must remain stage right, but Dawn, as Maria's voice, must somehow reach stage left *and* change costume. Further, she must do both unobtrusively. If the transition fails, it will snap the audience out of whatever reverie the scene is capable of, much like the awkwardness of a jump cut in film.

Assigning parts to the interpreters quickly turns to an exercise in futility. Of the original interpreters who'd shown up to the first rehearsal, only Andi Kreps remains. Diane's conception has always been to match gender where possible and then to hand out parts in descending order of ability, so that speaking actors with the most lines would be paired with the most experienced interpreters. By early March, Andi appears to be handling virtually every role simultaneously. This is not an impossibility, but it is a far cry from what Diane wants to achieve—a show that integrates the interpreters into the action as a whole and doesn't relegate them into a secondary status as multipersonality onlookers.

Solo interpreting for either theater or public events is known as platform interpreting. Platform is the style seen during the Super Bowl halftime shows, or as an accompaniment to the national anthem at sporting events. Andi has personal experience as a platform interpreter, but only with public speakers, not theater. In any event, she agrees with Diane that platform interpreting would be totally inappropriate for a blended cast like *West Side Story*'s. The immediate solution is to give even more responsibility to Jen Harris and Anna Poplett. Jen has plenty to do already as Riff's girlfriend, Velma, and has also been cast as a chorus voice for the Shark girls. Anna, who nearly landed the choice job of singing the role of Maria, has wound up as a generic Jet girl and chorus singer. Now, drafted as an interpreter, her stage time almost doubles. Anna is a junior Deaf Education major, but her ASL is not yet as advanced as Andi's or Carrie's. When either Andi or Carrie attempt to give advice, Anna resists, forcing Diane to run interference between the three, mollifying and stroking various bruised egos. It doesn't help that Carrie and Anna are roommates—and they have not been getting along.

Andi has her own problems. She initially heard about the *West Side Story* project through rumors at ISD, where she works, and eventually received a phone call from Carrie, asking if she would be interested in signing on (pun intended). Andi agreed, but never expected to be the most experienced interpreter involved. After two other student interpreters dropped out early in the rehearsal process, Andi begins to feel that the weight of the entire show rests squarely on her shoulders. It is not a situation she relishes.

Andi Kreps lives with a golden retriever puppy named Finley on the first floor of a spacious two-story white house just one large block from Mac's campus, a campus she graduated from in 1998 with a Deaf Ed degree. The rooms are clean, airy, and decorated with a tendency toward country crafts and incense candles; the largest art print is Bouguereau's *The Nut Gatherers*, showing two young girls contentedly at play. Andi herself is petite, with a long, Nordic ponytail. In cold weather, she has a penchant for bulky gray sweatshirts bearing the block-lettered names of various colleges, notably Mac and Gallaudet. She drives a sporty black Ford Escort with a spoiler on the trunk and a license plate reading "ASL 75," the number referring to the year she was born. Since graduating, she has worked regularly at ISD in the school's evaluation center, a job funded by a research grant from Gallaudet. Andi, with others, tracks the progress of ISD graduates, assesses how and what they're doing, and logs the results with an eye toward improving ISD's curriculum. The only way to get better at interpreting, she explains, is "to push yourself, to be immersed" in the culture. Her desire to improve was the primary reason she agreed to do *West Side Story*, but, from the beginning, she questions whether she is capable of living up to the job. Somewhat ruefully, she admits there are many interpreters better qualified than herself; she often dreams that she could be as good as they.

On paper—that is to say, officially—Andi's qualifications are through the state of Illinois and the state's major test, the Interpretive Skills Assessment Screening (ISAS). Illinois offers the test, like other standardized tests such as the SAT or ACT, several times a year at various sites around the state. The first segment is a written multiple-choice exam that takes about a half hour. It covers certain basic factual information and a series of ethical dilemmas such as, what to do if the person you are interpreting for launches into a dirty and probably offensive joke? Different interpreters field different answers, but the official response is to interpret the joke verbatim. Other questions often deal with issues of confidentiality. Interpreters enjoy (or are strapped by) the equivalent of the doctor-patient privilege, which is to say that what passes in private between a person and his or her interpreter may remain exclusively with them. The written ISAS test seeks to reveal gaps in a prospective interpreter's cultural or ethical training, and those who stray too often from the correct answers will not be invited to take the interview portion of the ISAS.

Andi took her interview exam in Chicago, with a friend along for support. The test takes two hours and consists of four segments. The first segment confronts the applicant with a video of a person signing in ASL, and the viewer must translate the ASL into spoken English. A video camera records the applicant's work for judging by a panel at a later date. The next segment reverses the situation, leaving the applicant to turn the tape's spoken English into ASL. This concludes the "interpreting" portion of the exam, and leads directly—no breaks allowed—to the transliterating section.

Transliterating is the proper term for much of what interpreters do because it may be defined as any translation that switches between manual and spoken language, yet does not change the language base, as would an ASL-to-English translation. Transliterating typically uses manual communication "to convey, in English word order, the message as it originates from the speaker," which in practical terms, makes it very close to CASE.[1] The transliterating interpreter uses signed English but drops word endings like "-ing" or "-ly" that have no exact ASL translation, then simultaneously and silently mouths the resulting words. Like the first portion of the exam, the test is given by videotape, then taped in turn; also like the first portion, the applicant has to translate in both directions—that is, first from transliterated sign into speech, then from speech into transliterated sign. It is not an easy test, any more than ASL itself is easy to master.

Andi arrived at Mac in a freshman class containing no less than forty-five declared Deaf Ed majors. Of those, only twelve survived the program to graduate with Deaf Education degrees. She credits this attrition to a failure to realize that not only is ASL difficult, but that Deaf Education still involves *education*. "It's like being a teacher plus," she says. "You go through all the teacher training, and on top of that, you have to learn at least one foreign language."

Still, Andi labels herself as an interpreting novice, and when doing freelance work, charges appropriately—twenty-five dollars an hour, with a two-hour minimum. The IRS treats interpreting work as a form of independent contracting, so no taxes are taken out for freelance jobs; much like a temp for companies like Kelly Services or Manpower, Andi must set aside about a quarter of her freelance paychecks for tax day. Still, interpreting work is both lucrative and educational, and she takes extra jobs as they come up, often interpreting for guest lecturers at ISD.

Even with such additional experience under her belt, Andi still feels unready for the next level of testing, which is given by the Registry of Interpreters for the Deaf (RID). Nor is she confident that she could pass every state's test, because many states give exams that differ from the Illinois test. Some states, rather than relying on a single exam, offer graduated testing that proceeds through various levels of competency. If an interpreter passes the tests in one state and then wants to work in another, he or she must first check with that state's certification board and make sure that their qualifications will be recognized. The state in question has the right to ask the interpreter to be tested again, this time using the new state's examination, much as drivers moving to California or Indiana must retake their driver's license exam. Similarly, national certification is possible, the RID being the only widely accepted certifying body. An interpreter accredited by several states or nationally certified is sometimes spoken of as well credentialed.

Andi's initial apprehension at working on *West Side Story* turns, in March, to enormous frustration precisely because the show lacks a well-credentialed interpreter. The most qualified people directly involved—Christopher Smith and Becky Cline, who isn't always available—will not be on the stage. Christopher could not be of much help in any event; Andi is perfectly aware that, novice or not, she has a more thorough knowledge of ASL than does Christopher, who was raised in a decidedly oral environment by hearing parents. Nor is Christopher always present when Andi needs him; not only does he have his hands completely full with updates in his choreography, but rehearsals continue to be split between several different rooms, which leaves Andi and Christopher separated, often for hours at a time.

Other potentially helpful people such as the ISD dorm parents (they escort the ISD contingent every night), appear uninterested and spend much of their time in the back rows or out in the hallway, counting the minutes until it's time to leave. One dorm parent, however, proves to be a lifesaving resource for Andi. Elsbietta Kaminski is a recent Polish immigrant, making her—very nearly, at least—a real-life Jet girl. She watches each rehearsal that she attends with an expression both severe and delighted, as if each mistake or miscue pains her personally. When Andi gets well and truly stuck on an individual word or phrase, she turns increasingly to Elsbietta for advice. One line in particular causes her fits, where Anybodys describes her prowess at creeping around the neighborhood. "I'm very good with shadows, you know," she says. "I sneak in and out like wind through a fence!" Andi already has a translation in mind but remains unhappy with it. Elsbietta offers a more direct, more graceful series of signs, most of which survive into the eventual performances. If nothing else, Elsbietta gives Andi the sense that she has not been completely abandoned. Abandonment, however, is not Andi's chief concern. Her worries center on who will bear ultimate responsibility for the final product.

In the meantime, there is nothing for it but to soldier on, with or without a male interpreter for Tony. With the only male interpreter that the show ever had long since gone, so Andi has to cover Tony's lines, as well as those of Riff, A-Rab, Doc, and Schrank. The unfortunate result is that Andi—thanks to a plethora of scenes that include pairings like Tony and Riff or Tony and Doc—frequently appears to be conversing with herself. Anna Poplett takes the parts of Krupke, Action, Anybodys, and Velma. (Velma, as played by Jen Harris, could potentially sign for herself, but it makes no theatrical sense for her to do so; Jen's character, Velma, has no more idea how to sign than she does how to improve on being a gang leader's moll.) Allison Titus, an interpreter who joins the cast at the same time as Ken Roumpos, adopts Diesel, Baby John, and Graziella—all of whom are hearing, which allows Allison to become the only sign interpreter to avoid specific duties as a voice interpreter. Anna handles the speaking and singing parts of Shark girl Rosalia, and Andi covers Glad Hand's lines. Jen Harris, who takes the voice parts of Francisca, has the same basic duties, except that Francisca has no spoken lines, only sung lyrics, a fact that leads to an eventual oversight in the program, where Jen's name does not appear in the cast list of voice interpreters.

Voice interpreting is not necessarily an easy task onstage, even with fixed and memorized dialogue. Sight lines become a major issue, especially in the largest scene, "Dance at the Gym." Glad Hand, who is played by a deaf actor, presents particular problems, because Glad Hand keeps separating the two warring factions by stepping in between them. Andi, off to the side, can't see when Glad Hand begins to sign. No matter where Andi goes, she can't quite see every move Glad Hand makes, and as a result, she often begins her speaking either too early or too late.

One attempted solution—to place Andi up above the action, on one of the scaffolds—is quickly abandoned, because she not only has to voice during the scene, but she also has to translate spoken English back to ASL due to the presence of Riff, A-Rab, and Schrank. It's a no-win situation for Diane—and, she worries, for the audience. With the interpreting pool apparently exhausted, someone will have to get short shrift. Glad Hand's lines—and the process of syncing them up with Andi—become the scene's sacrificial lamb by virtue of sound's ability to travel indiscriminately. Better, Diane decides, to keep Andi clearly visible for deaf audiences than to give her a bird's-eye view for the hearing. One way or another, the hearing audience will pick up Glad Hand's lines—even if they are a little off the mark.

In general, the voice interpreters match up to their deaf counterparts simply through the needs of the score and not necessarily because of any physical resemblance. Matt Fraas, for example, can handle bass and baritone notes, and thus he becomes CJ's (Bernardo's) speaking and singing voice. Meredith and Olivia may be near opposites in skin color (Meredith is white and Olivia, black), and their visual relationship may not be clear, but Meredith can hit the notes required. Diane decides to trust that the audience, through visual cues like blocking and costume, will learn to figure it out.

Costuming a musical in which most of the performers use sign presents all the standard problems of costuming a show and then some. Jen Harris, a senior Deaf Ed major who has stayed an extra semester specifically to be in *West Side Story*, takes on the task of costuming the cast. She has no experience with this and ropes in Meredith Blair as an assistant. Meredith, who over the summer of 1999 told Diane that she wanted "to be involved in every way possible," quits the job every two weeks or so, citing her impossibly busy schedule. Jen lures her back, time and time again, simply by asking Meredith's opinion about each new piece as she adds it to the wardrobe.

Jen hopes to give each gang a distinct personality without sacrificing visibility, specifically the visibility of hand motions. "The first rule for interpreters," Jen confides, "is don't wear patterns." It's a rule that carries over to educators of deaf students everywhere. Grappling with too many colors, lines, or swirls is a surefire recipe for a headache, and the longer one has to focus on a chiaroscuro of hands and clothes, the worse the effects. Many of Mac's Deaf Edders sport closets full of solids, with nary a pattern in sight. Pants and skirts are less important because most signing takes place well above the waist, but the same guidelines still apply.

In costuming *West Side Story*, Jen, Meredith, and Diane start with the Jets. Meredith sees them as skaters, but has trouble describing what that means. When she and Jen shop together, the spoken English word *skaters* still fails to clarify anything, so they switch into ASL, and then things suddenly make more sense. The Jets will be a little grungy, definitely more Americanized. They'll wear khakis, dark T-shirts and a variety of printed button-downs over the top. Patterns on the Jets won't be a problem, because none of them have to sign or interpret.

Not surprisingly, the Jets turn out to be the easy side of the equation. Everyone involved in costuming sees the Sharks as slick, savvy dressers, but agreeing on exactly what that means in practical terms is slippery, hard to pin down. Meredith and Jen clip magazine photographs to demonstrate their take on "hoochie" clothes—shirts that leave the midriff bare, slinky fabrics, shiny vinyl—but never work up either sketch drawings or a consistent color palette. Jen is tall with thick, shoulder-length brown hair; she's well-spoken and exudes a definitive confidence that lulls Diane into a false sense of security. Diane, too caught up in the production's other needs, forgets entirely that Jen has never done costumes before, and has very little idea of what the job traditionally entails. She leaves Jen to her own devices, imagining—correctly, as it turns out—that Jen will learn to swim, one way or another.

Linking interpreters to their primary characters proves to be an even more significant challenge. Andi, Anna, and Allison, interpreters one and all, are easy enough. Jen issues each a basic black top and, as most of their visible duties will involve interpreting for the Jets, khaki pants to match. Costuming Meredith is trickier because she has to switch in and out of the role of Anybodys and become, sometimes in a matter of seconds, the voice of Anita. She ends up in knee-length parachute-style shorts, covered in pockets and topped with a grayish shirt. A torn olive vest goes over the shirt, almost as loaded with pockets as are the shorts. When she voices for Anita, she removes the vest, which quickly matches her to Anita's basic silver top.

Meredith (now back to playing Anybodys) also illustrates the next level of costuming, where each character matches up to a girlfriend or boyfriend within their gang. Throughout the show, Anybodys carries a bright orange scarf dangling from her side pocket, her sole concession to girlhood; the boy she eventually falls for is Action, and his outer shirt is bright orange. Similarly, Riff's T-shirt is a deep bloodred, and to link Velma to Riff, Jen gives herself a pink top. Onstage, Jen also provides a voice for Shark girl Francisca; Francisca wears a tight-fitting baby blue pullover with a feathery ruffle at the collar, so Jen adds a light blue button-down to her own costume to provide the audience with a visual cue that she and Francisca go together. To keep her connection to Riff equally alive, she leaves the top shirt unbuttoned so the pink beneath continues to show.

Finding costumes for Pearlene proves to be the hardest job of all, even though matching her with Dawn Williams is not difficult. One costume after another fails, making Pearlene look, in Meredith's words, "skanky." Pearlene, as Maria, needs three basic costumes, and the first and most troublesome of these is a dress for Anita to convert onstage from "a dress for kneeling at the altar" to "a dress for dancing." The exceptionally light blue dress that finally works is as thin as lingerie, and Pearlene is not

100 percent comfortable with how revealing it is, especially above the waist. Nor is it dark enough for Pearlene's own light skin tones. Jen decides the best solution is to dye the fabric. As luck would have it, the dress is nylon, and the only dyes available clearly warn against use on nylon, because the dye will eat through the fabric and destroy it. Desperate, Jen calls her mother, who has far more experience with sewing and fabric. Her mother suggests using a natural method. "Try dark grape juice," she advises, and Jen runs to the store for ten little cans of frozen grape concentrate. The next morning, with Pearlene's dress hanging over the tub, the juice dye appears to have worked. The dress is violet, a lovely, evenly distributed color—but when Jen goes to touch it, the dress turns out to be sticky. Panicked, she calls her mother again, who muses that it should be safe to wash the dress, that the color will hold. It does not. The grape-based violet bleeds away so completely that the dress returns to its original near-white color. No further attempts are made to alter the fabric, and the dress, light or not, turns out to be a permanent part of the show.

One doubled job that becomes unexpectedly trying is Carrie Moore's. Diane and Carrie have planned since December '99 for Carrie to work as both a rehearsal interpreter and as the stage manager, but neither foresaw how difficult this would turn out to be. As stage manager, Carrie is a person invested with authority; she has charge of remembering what has already been blocked and rehearsed, and adding notes on both subjects to the script. Stage managers inform actors of when they've missed lines or cues, when they're using the wrong prop, and when they're facing or moving in the wrong direction. Stage managers' responsibilities grow and expand as the show becomes tighter, better rehearsed.

Unfortunately, Carrie also serves as a de facto interpreter, especially when Becky Cline, hired officially to be Diane's personal interpreter, is not available. When wearing her interpreter's hat, Carrie is required to be objective, neutral. She cannot do this and still maintain her supervisory status as stage manager. The job becomes an impossible compromise, reducing both her authority and her efficiency as a conduit for communication. Little by little, her standing erodes; the adversarial relationships that soon develop between Carrie and many members of the cast cause black moods and frequent recriminations. Diane, all too aware that something is wrong, wishes she could relieve Carrie of her interpreting duties, but has no one else to fall back on. She begins to wonder if only a Deaf director should attempt to direct deaf actors—much less deaf and hearing actors engaged in a musical. Her rational side discards the thought again and again, but she cannot quite shake it. Has she bitten off more than she can chew? Is a deaf musical, by its very nature, an impossibility?

Quintet
(Tonight Medley)

The subject is not beautiful, but what *West Side Story* draws out of it is beautiful. For it has a searching point of view.

Brooks Atkinson[1]

Webster's Encyclopedic Unabridged Dictionary defines *cacophony* as: 1. a harsh discordance of sound; dissonance; 2. a discordant and meaningless mixture of different sounds; 3. *Music.* Frequent use of discords of a harshness and relationship difficult to understand.[2]

What Leonard Bernstein evidently had in mind for the complex medley "Quintet" was a triumphal blend of the musical themes driving the individual characters. As they sing the quintet, each character, for personal reasons, looks forward to "Tonight." The resulting music is indeed cacophonous, beautifully so—despite Carrie Moore's blunt description of it as "the worst song in the whole show"—and it soars, both in terms of octaves and effect, to spectacular heights. It is also, according to Diane, "an abject failure for deaf audiences," a fact for which she blames herself. And yet, Bernstein, Sondheim, and company surely never had a deaf audience in mind while creating this music, and the visual cacophony created around their "Quintet" would have seemed, for them, only natural. For a deaf audience, it is an entirely different animal.

The scene opens with Charlie Smerz (Riff) and his interpreter, Andi, perched high on the farthest back left scaffolding, singing and signing the opening lines. A single spotlight catches their movements and colors their faces. So far, deaf and hearing audiences are on equal footing, since the visuals are in immediate proximity to the sounds. Then a second spotlight picks out CJ (Bernardo) and his voicer, Matt Fraas. These two appear downstage right, but again, deaf and hearing viewers still are given equal access, because by now, Charlie has stopped singing. After a few more exchanges, however, the call-and-response becomes a full-blown duet, and now the deaf audience members must make an active choice between following either CJ or Andi. It is virtually impossible to make sense of both at once. The medley blossoms further as Olivia (Anita) and her voicer, Meredith, step into the light on a scaffold set upstage center. A three-way sing-along quickly shifts to four parts as Ken (Tony) enters, backed by his interpreter. They stride into a new light focused downstage center. Finally, Pearlene (Maria) joins in with Dawn, ensconced on Maria's back left balcony. The bottom line: The deaf audience cannot possibly track each of the five signers, and thus they lose perhaps four-fifths of the scene's text, its lyricized story. And, because they can only participate in half of the available cacophany (the visuals) to start with, they are essentially reduced to experiencing approximately one-tenth of what the scene is capable of producing.

When an observer points this out to Diane, it proves to be a moment of truth, a real crisis. She feels that she has worked long and hard to create a show that is easily accessible to both hearing and deaf audiences, yet here she faces a scene that, from its very inception, cannot work for both audiences simultaneously. The staging only exacerbates the problem. Would it make sense, she wonders, to bring all the interpreters together, to one central point? Or reblock the entire scene? In the end, she leaves the medley well enough alone, partly because of time constraints and partly because the sheer look of the scene turns out to be exceptionally effective. Still, her failure to completely integrate the needs of the two audiences haunts her right through to the close of the show, and all negative comments from Deaf community members lead her back, inexorably, to the staging of "Quintet." How could it have been improved, mounted differently? Was there a key she left undiscovered?

Ironically, when the *Jacksonville Journal-Courier* runs its feature story on the Thursday before opening night, the picture they choose is a wide-angle shot of the medley scene, with all the performer's arms outstretched in vivid, passionate sign. As a photograph, it's a marvelous, eerie tableau. Even so, Diane cannot not help but feel the sting. "Of course they chose that," she grouses. "It's the only scene that *can't* work."

As of late February 2000, four parts remain to be cast, all with one common tie: they are roles expressly written for adults. *West Side Story* contains a Greek chorus of sorts in the form of Doc, the elderly, ineffective druggist, together with the bitter police lieutenant, Schrank, and his bully of a sidekick, Officer Krupke. Glad Hand rounds out the group. As the teenagers around them hurtle ever closer to tragedy, the best these four can manage are futile orders and tame advice. Doc, attempting to chew out the Jets at large, sums up his frustration by crying, "You make this world lousy!" Action, in a rare moment of perception, responds with, "That's the way we found it, Doc." It's the line in the play that best sums up the enormous cultural divide between *West Side Story*'s teen "stars" and the adults who might, in a more affectionate world, have offered guidance.

Enter Richard W. Fee. Richard is a recent transplant to Jacksonville whose last post was at the Idaho School for the Deaf and Blind. One year after an initial interview at Mac, Richard agreed to take a second look—an event which prompted Dean Jim Goulding to ask, "Richard, if we fly you out here again, will you take the job?" The job in question is a combination platter, for Richard serves as both an associate professor and as Director of the Deaf and Hard of Hearing Teacher Education program. Ironically, the position he assumes is the one formerly filled by ousted Ruth-Ann Hecker; in fact, had he taken the initial job offer in 1998, Ruth-Ann would never have worked for Mac or had any contact whatsoever with Diane and her nascent steering committee. As of February 2000, Richard himself has hardly done more than touch base with Diane or the *West Side Story* production. This seems particularly odd given that his primary focus in taking the Mac job continues to be improving communication, not just within the department but from the department outward. Looking back, he remembers meeting Diane soon after arriving on campus (in January, 1999), and learning, in vague terms, about *West Side Story*. Then came the summer break, followed quickly by another busy semester. *West Side Story*, despite being run out of the very same building that contains Richard's office, felt to him like something distinctly apart. Moreover, very few of the seventy-odd Deaf Ed majors on campus were involved. As far as Richard could see, he and *West Side Story* were simply on different and not necessarily parallel paths.

Diane, however, sees things quite differently. On a campus as small as Mac's, she remains surprised that the entire Deaf Ed department hasn't leapt at the chance to involve themselves. The students' reticence is perplexing, and by the time rehearsals get under way, she begins to assume, however tacitly, that she will not be getting any help from that quarter, that the department has, en masse, turned its back on the whole enterprise. To a large extent, Diane feels that the Deaf Education Department—and to a much lesser degree, ISD—has been downright negligent. After all, she is in desperate need of interpreters, and the Deaf

Education Department is in desperate need of proving grounds for its majors. Yet somehow, the two have passed in the night.

Nor have the deaf members of *West Side Story*'s steering committee taken an active role, or even made many recommendations. Bob Dramin has just welcomed his new son into the world and has no spare time to devote to this or any other play. (Bob is particularly proud that both of his children, like himself, are profoundly deaf; they are the fifth successive generation in his family to be without hearing.) Paula Chance is still sick, out of touch. Chuck Nash can barely keep up with the job he has, and Diane has tried hard not to lean on him any more than she has to. His main task remains getting the students back and forth from rehearsals via the dorm parents. Cara Hammond's role has become, increasingly, one of logistical coordinator and contact person. She did unearth Kevin Healy, a potential interpreter for Tony, but cannot not find a replacement when Kevin drops out.

For his part, Richard Fee has a new and demanding job, one still fresh enough that it requires a certain day-to-day acclimation. To make matters worse, he has inherited a department that, until recently, has done little to communicate within itself—a situation Richard has attempted to rectify with a constant barrage of "Fee-mails," a derisive but affectionate term the students use for his ongoing blitzkrieg of e-mail messages.

Effective as it is, e-mail can never replace good old-fashioned happenstance. Richard finally discovered that Bob Dramin is a member of *West Side Story*'s steering committee—and that Diane has a steering committee—in the late summer of 1999 when Bob popped a tape of *Bye Bye Birdie* into the department's audiovisual equipment and neglected to adjust the volume (for a hearing person) to a tolerable level. Bob's office is only one door down from Richard's, and when Richard burst in and demanded to know what all the noise was about, Bob pointed to the screen, indicating one of the lead dancers. "That's Christopher Smith," he said. "He choreographed this. He's very good."

Richard, who had never heard of Christopher Smith, had no idea why he should care about a somewhat outdated Chicago production of a musical; nor could he immediately comprehend why Bob, as a Deaf man, would take a sudden work-related interest in American musical theater. Bob explained that *West Side Story* was in preproduction, but that turned out to be almost the last piece of information, for months, that Richard heard about the show. It wasn't until the first auditions rolled around in November that Richard finally met Christopher. Even that meeting produced nothing in the way of cooperation, despite the best intentions of both the Drama and Deaf Ed departments.

Now, with three weeks of rehearsals already gone, Diane concludes that the lack of adult cast members is sufficiently problematic to warrant a plea for help during a meeting of the general faculty. Toward the end of the meeting, she stands up, not very far from tears, and tells the assemblage that she is "almost desperate" for help. She remembers asking for performers—in particular, adult actors willing to play the four adult roles—but when Richard approaches her after the meeting, he expects only to volunteer for managing the ticket sales or helping with the sets. Diane takes one look at Richard and asks if he will take the part of Lieutenant Schrank. Richard, whose last stage appearance was in 1964 (he played Professor Kokintz in *The Mouse That Roared*), says yes before he can fully grasp what he has committed to. It then takes him weeks to reveal to his colleagues that he has an active role in the play. Terrified that he'll "bomb out," he tells no one except his family.

Richard has red hair, a rarity in the Jacksonville area, and he keeps it neatly parted just above his left ear. His smile is shy and ready; when pushed a little harder, the smile widens and joins with a quiet, pensive laugh. He is not a man who yells or abuses teenagers—even hoodlums. If he has a temper, and everyone says he does not, he certainly never shows it. Lieutenant Schrank is his polar opposite, a man who has dedicated his life to arm-twisting and forcing his will on others. He's a man with a chip on his shoulder and an ulcer in his gut.

If Richard and Schrank have any similarities, it would be in their offices. One can easily imagine Schrank with a map of the five boroughs—or at least the upper West Side—pinned to the wall just above his metal desk, and sure enough, Richard Fee has a large road map of Illinois stapled to an old bulletin board, just above an equally aged and, for Mac, standard-issue metal desk. Black filing cabinets lay claim to most of the available floor space, just as they surely would in Schrank's world. But would Schrank keep a copy of *The Bell Curve* on hand? Richard Fee does, along with a Coca-Cola clock, round and perilously close to falling off its temporary resting place atop one of the aforementioned filing cabinets. Richard's shelves also hold an enormous black-bound tome ominously entitled, *The Disability Handbook*. One doubts that Schrank would even admit a copy into the room.

Typecasting, however, is not on Diane's mind one way or the other, at least insomuch as it affects asking Richard to play Schrank. With very few options left, she takes whomever she can get, as quickly as possible, and Richard is a live body—and, better yet, a live body who can sign. To a point. Richard, despite three decades of experience as a Deaf Ed teacher and administrator, is not proficient in ASL. He can communicate using a limited version of ASL, and he understands most of what ASL users say to him, but that is as far as he can go. Signed English and CASE are much more his line. This, however, turns out to be a blessing. From the get-go, Diane has always thought of Schrank as a man whose clumsy signing arouses the active scorn of the ultrahip Sharks. With Richard in the role, her conception of Schrank's imperfect signing becomes an instant reality. Meredith, watching Richard rehearse, notes sourly that she too was typecast. A crew member's response: "Learn to live with it. You only have two types of casting: typecasting and casting against type." In Richard's case, thanks to his absolutely negligible mean streak, Diane has managed both at once.

The pressure to perform (both literally and figuratively) is enormous for Richard. He doesn't want to let down the students who've worked so hard already on the show, and he's all too aware that he's joining the process late in the game. More frightening, at least for him, is the prospect of letting down the deaf audience. He knows, perhaps better than any hearing person working the show, that deaf audiences naturally track to movement. Visual cues and strong motion will draw attention away from what would otherwise be the central actions on stage. In Schrank's scenes, Schrank signs for himself and thus has no need for an interpreter; to Richard's mind, this suggests that all eyes, quite literally, will be on him. Also, he doubts that ASL and speech can ever really be matched, that the lines of the play will necessarily entail editing and erroneous translation before they can be spoken for the deaf audience. Thus, given his character's inherent sloppiness to consider, Richard faces a double-edged sword: how best to convey Schrank's contempt (which would surely come out in sign) while still making what he says absolutely clear?

The solution, insofar as Diane and Richard ever solve this dilemma, is to have Richard-as-Schrank speak and sign very slowly, as if the mere act of translating his speech into sign causes him to perform both actions in choppy fits and starts. It's a discomfiting departure from the quick, fluid signing attained by the rest of the signing cast, and it has the effect of separating Schrank from everyone else, both hearing and deaf, making him (and not the Sharks or Jets) the consummate outsider. Again, Richard himself fits the analogy. As a hearing man charged with educating students on how to reach the Deaf, Richard melds perfectly into neither community. He signs, but cannot use ASL; he hears, but makes his living in the realm of the deaf. As he launches himself into the production, he tells himself that he has to do well, not just for his own sake, but for the sake of his program, for Deaf Ed at Mac. If he does well—if the show does well—it will lend prestige to Deaf Ed in general. If either one fails, it will only confirm the Deaf community's all-too-common impression that hearing people are just a bunch of insensitive, Schrankish jerks.

As for the overall involvement of the Deaf Ed department, everything changes from the moment Richard accepts his onstage role. He meets with Anna Poplett (his student worker) immediately to get a feel for what has been done so far and what is coming. He learns from her that the show is still short on interpreters, and quickly sends Diane a reassuring e-mail in which he states, "I didn't realize the run-around [*sic*] you got from people. Deaf Ed majors should be lining up to help." Above and beyond his departmental duties, Richard quickly becomes a one-man publicity machine, announcing the production to meetings of deaf educators around the state, and sending out daily updates to various e-mail lists nationwide. He snaps endless pictures of the rehearsals, then posts them on Mac's Deaf Ed homepage, which becomes a virtual conduit for the Deaf community to familiarize themselves with the production. One morning, with a few clicks of his mouse, he sends out an announcement for the upcoming show to fifteen thousand separate e-mail addresses. Calls and requests for tickets begin to pour in from as far away as St. Louis and Champaign/Urbana, and Diane realizes that she will have to establish a protocol for ticket sales, a problem Mac has not had to address in almost two decades. Diane's first Mac production drew as few as eight people a night. Now, she begins to suspect that *West Side Story* will not only sell out, but it will do so weeks before the house ever opens.

The February 2000 faculty meeting produces two more out-of-the-woodwork actors, and within days, the roles of Doc and Krupke are filled. Krupke, a famous but small role, goes to Jeannie Zeck, another Mac newcomer, an Assistant Professor of English who spent the last several years teaching at Susquehanna College in Pennsylvania. She has a wealth of acting experience under her belt, and even in casual speech, she keeps her voice carefully modulated. Her words sound almost clipped, as if she seeks to savor every last consonant and vowel. Around the rim of her basement office, which sits just across the hall and one door down from Diane's, she displays a collection of hats, mostly women's. The hats hang in a neat, single row and manage to dominate the hordes of textbooks beneath. As Krupke, Jeannie turns out to be almost dangerously deliberate—or deliberately dangerous. In her hands, a police whistle becomes incisive, something to be aimed. Although an interpreter always conveys the blowing whistle to the deaf segment of the audience, it's never quite the same; police the world over could learn a thing or two about whistle-blowing from Jeannie "Krupke" Zeck.

Jay Peterson, Mac's long-time Professor of Music, agrees—with some reluctance—to play Doc. Initially, he said he would take the much more modest role of Krupke, but Diane coaxes him gently into Doc's larger shoes with a pungent combination of sincere flattery and outright begging. Jay turns out to be an over-the-top performer, an actor who escapes being a ham by a hairbreadth. Still, he gets his lines and his blocking down quickly and turns his obvious Doc-like traits—short stature, gray and thinning hair, a temporarily injured arm—into immediate assets. Like Richard Fee, Jay has not been on the theatrical stage in almost thirty years. He is no stranger, however, to the stage itself. He once toured Europe as a concert organist and still gives annual recitals, often featuring the music of J. S. Bach, at Mac's Annie Merner Chapel. He can be prickly, and former students (Terri Benz, for example) say that, whereas most people tend to accept new acquaintances until they have a reason to dislike them, Jay is quite the opposite. New faces are likely to receive, if not a cold shoulder, no real attention at all. Once he gives his friendship, however, he is famously loyal. He and his wife, Cheryl, together with three other couples, have held gourmet banquets for over twenty-five years. Hosting duties rotate but everyone contributes dishes. The meals often cover seven courses, opening with complicated hors d'oeuvres and capped by elaborate, exotic desserts. Outsiders are never invited.

In the first three weeks of January 2000, Jay and Diane served as faculty organizers and chaperones for a student trip to Bali. For Diane, those weeks were the first in over seven months that could have been described as pain-free; by the time she returned, her fibromyalgia could (almost) be relegated to the status of a distant memory. Jay, who had been to Bali before, did virtually all the grunt work and set up most of the organized activities and tours, including lessons in gamelan and traditional dance. Diane, who is used to organizing everything for herself, felt like an extra, and sometimes superfluous, wheel. Still, she seized on the chance to relax and even managed to drag a best friend from high school along with her. The entire experience was overwhelmingly positive, and it was on Bali that she finally got to know Ken Roumpos, Matt Fraas, and Allison Titus, all of whom joined her cast in short order. (Other cast members who took the trip include Meredith Blair and Jennifer Harris. At times, *West Side Story*'s rehearsals resemble a somewhat premature Bali trip reunion.)

Neither Jay nor Jeannie know more than the most rudimentary sign language, picked up, if at all, from frequent interactions with Mac's many Deaf Ed majors. While this does nothing to harm the overall conception of the show (where only Glad Hand and Schrank, of the adults, can sign at all), it does little to integrate them into the cast. The ISD actors, who are finally comfortable with the majority of the hearing actors, never seem to warm to any of the new arrivals. Diane decides it doesn't matter. Doc's shop is Jet territory, so the Sharks ought to feel uncomfortable around Doc. Krupke is a police officer, the United States as oppressor, full of rules, uniforms and not-so-subtle slights. Schrank is even worse.

And Glad Hand? With four weeks left until opening, the show still doesn't have a Glad Hand. (A deaf Mac student named Justin took the part originally, but then missed a key rehearsal, and when confronted the next day by Diane, he explained that he'd stayed in his dorm room because he felt "sad." Diane fired him, as gently as she could, on the spot.) Glad Hand has a small but crucial part in that he attempts, however feebly, to reach out to both of the rival gangs. And because Diane wants Glad Hand to use ASL, her choices are limited. Finally, she hits upon a local, boy-next-door solution: cast Christopher Smith. Christopher, thrilled and flattered beyond all reason at being offered a part, accepts immediately. He feels the role is "suitable" because "Glad Hand is so colorful, cheerful and over-patience." The gymnasium dance gets added back into the rehearsal schedule, this time—for the first time—with an actual Glad Hand to lead the actors through their traces. The dance at the gym begins to gel, and Diane allows herself to hope, finally, that things are looking up.

The Rumble

Hey Diane, I had a conversation with Becky Cline today to discuss about the students attitude. They got the "funky attitude" especially Joey when he is sick of doing "over and over and over". So I think we need to bring it up tonight before rehearsal. They need to understand the "over, over, and over" is part of theatre processing. I remembered my drama teacher and choreographer back in my old teen days kept saying... "You will be hearing the same lecture in more than one thousand times in your lifetime even the professional actors, dancers, and singers have to hear the same the lecture."

Christopher Smith
E-mail dated 3/9/00

Fighting: the need to fight, and ways to avoid it are, to Diane, still central to the entire *West Side Story* project, even though the early objections about gangs have subsided. She understands why many people choose to focus on the violence that drives so much of the story, but finds that, for her, the appeal of *West Side Story* lies elsewhere. She prefers to perceive the world in dialectical terms, and accordingly, she cannot imagine violence without peace or hatred without love—and it is love, its power, its inherent optimism, that has held her attention from the start. As she tells the *Jacksonville Journal-Courier* in an April 6 feature, "If people fight because they don't understand each other, they fall in love because they do."

Combat, however, is the name of the game when it comes to rehearsing first "The Prologue" and then "The Rumble," the fatal brawl between the Sharks and the Jets that ends with both gangs' leaders, Riff and Bernardo, stabbed to death on the street. Stage combat, usually done so badly, is often—even at its best—a painful thing to watch. Here, thanks in equal parts to Christopher's choreography, Diane's pedagogical skills, and the actors' willingness to fling themselves around the stage, the rumble seems surprisingly real, even at the necessarily close range imposed by the black box space. When Bernardo first hits the ground, viewers can feel the concussion right through the floorboards. But night after night, the fight goes off without any significant injury or hitch. In one dress rehearsal, a pair of glasses goes flying, but the next night, the costume department adds an athletic strap to the wardrobe list. In another, A-Rab (Prentice Southwell) and Pepe (Patrick Baker) skid on a milk crate and crash through the silver-painted blinds closing off Doc's shop; the solid wood of the soda fountain counter comes dangerously close to denting Patrick's skull. At moments like these, the genie of real violence nearly escapes the bottle. Pulse rates rise; the threat, as Riff says of the Sharks, is large.

Diane leads the actors by the nose through their stage combat instruction, going step by cautious step, building from the ground up. The first rule: Always establish eye contact. Never make a move without the permission of your combat partner. She insists that sparring partners must develop signals that indicate, "Okay, go ahead"—and if that signal gets forgotten or is not given for any reason, the only option is to abort the attack. The second rule demands that the defender must always have total control of the action, even in such offensive schemes as punching, kicking, or pummeling. The Sharks, well schooled in making up hand signals, quickly invent a series of gestures and eye fakes to cue their Jet counterparts. Even so, the fighting initially resembles something careful and cautious, a ballet of feints and

jabs without the menacing thump and noise of a real fight. Trying to add spice to the combat, Diane attempts to demonstrate a
more involved maneuver, a throw and drop that leaves her on her
back on the floor. Once there, she finds she can't get up. "Help!"
she cries. "I'm too pregnant to move!"

Pregnancy has been less of a burden in directing *West Side
Story* than she had expected. She has not experienced morning
sickness since the first trimester, and in tandem with the Bali
"vacation," the conclusion of those early months also brought
much-needed relief from the debilitating pain of fibromyalgia.
The creative high she gets from rehearsing carries her past the
general exhaustion of pregnancy itself, and except when called
upon to show off the basics of stage combat, she has not found
herself restricted in any way. In this, she considers herself to be
uncommonly lucky; at the peak of her FMS symptoms, she was
beginning to count herself as a person with a lasting, perhaps
insoluble handicap. She does not, however, believe that she has
gained any particular insight into the realm of deafness through
her own brush with disability. Deafness and pain management are
sufficiently different that she feels it would be immodest and bla-
tantly egotistical to assume that she has a better understanding of
a deaf person's world simply because she was, for a brief time,
forced to view the world through a new and different lens.

Stage combat, given her pregnancy, does leave her at a
decided disadvantage, and she leans ever harder on Christopher
and the actors to find that fine line between dance and realistic
battle, between risk and personal safety. Leonard Bernstein, in a
1957 interview with the *New York Herald Tribune*, recalled similar
difficulties in perfecting "The Rumble":

> The last scene of the first act is a typical West Side "rumble," a
> free-for-all knife fight between the two rival gangs. As Jerry
> (Jerome Robbins) staged it, the fight is as good, as frightening as
> any I've . . . seen in a Gary Cooper Western, and yet it's choreo-
> graphed to my music from beginning to end. That's where the

tightrope comes in. If the "rumble" had been too balletic, we would have fallen off to one side—all you'd have is just another ballet. And if it had been too realistic, we would have fallen off the other side—there would have been no poetry, no art. Now carry that example to every single detail in the show and you can understand why *West Side Story* was such hard work to put together . . .[1]

Joey Gillis (playing Chino) takes the lead in creativity. While the rest of the cast members involve themselves in more traditional moves like hair-pulling (easily controlled by the attackee), Joey and his opponent, Dane Vincent (Diesel), work out a complicated move whereby Joey leaps at Dane and Dane then spins under him, leaving Joey atop Dane's shoulders. Joey stands over six feet in height, but Dane is both bulky and strong, and he hoists Joey like a doll. For the coup de grâce, Dane swings Joey toward a network of rusted scaffolding and proceeds to pound Joey's head into the rails. Not once, not twice, not three times, but over and over again, Joey slams against the side rails, stopping himself just shy of a skull-splitting injury by means of his outstretched hands, invisible to the audience. It's a scene-stealing marvel, so successful that the real focus—Tony stabbing Bernardo—is all but lost, even though Bernardo's death occurs downstage and should, in theory, completely block Joey and Dane.

Joey proves to be a scene-stealer and a firebrand throughout. His stoner clothes would put him at home in the grungiest skateboard strip of Venice Beach, and his tasseled knit hats resemble those of an acid-wracked war protester from 1970. He vocalizes strongly when signing and always has a question or comment when Diane gives notes. His bleach-blonde hair and new goatee give him the air of a tall and belligerent pixie, a real prima donna in the making. Not long before spring break, Joey, unhappy with a critical note from Diane, dashes out of the room and races away down the hall. None of the dorm parents pursue him, so Diane, refusing to let him get away, gives chase. Only three months before her due date and very much out of shape, she has no hope of outrunning her quarry. Worse, she cannot yell at him to stop, as she might for a hearing actor.

Joey, who has no real desire to escape the building, eventually slows and waits for Diane to catch up. The conversation that ensues is fractured and understood more by implication than actual language, since Diane still cannot sign well enough to make specific points. She does insist, however, that Joey return to the theater space and follow through on his commitments. Joey, his feelings assuaged, agrees to return to rehearsal. It is neither his first nor his last transgression. A few days later, on a beautiful warm evening, he and three other ISD actors decide to walk the one-mile route to Mac rather than ride with the rest of the group in the ISD bus, a large white van with "Illinois School for the Deaf" painted in blue on the side. None of the four arrive on time, and the ISD dorm parents insist they did not see the boys along the straight line of College Avenue. Fuming, Diane lights into Joey when he arrives, which only turns him sulky. She eases her wrath when it comes to CJ and Joey's other walking companions. It turns out that CJ is embarrassed at having let Joey con him into a detour and a slow, ambling pace. Carrie later explains that CJ is a "good kid" who sometimes gets led into things, often by Joey, that he wouldn't normally do.

Joey's charisma and leadership are unstable at best. He takes any stage activity to the nth degree. Offstage, he can barely keep himself still. He makes for a fierce, snarling Chino, often at odds with the script. When entering, Joey arrives by literally flying over the top of a scaffold rail and leaping, with the ease of a manic gibbon, straight to the ground. This particular scaffold has its walkboards set at five feet, and Joey, by clearing the rail, makes it a minimum of a six-foot-six vertical. His verve (and his aerial entrances) prompt Diane to claim, more than once and to anyone who will listen, that "Joey could do the entire show by himself."

Diane, however, cannot mount the production by herself, and she has heard endless warnings—from ISD staff and faculty, from members of her steering committee, and even from Christopher—that "the deaf kids" have little comprehension of long-term commitment, that they have very short attention spans. Well before the advent of rehearsals, Diane took the unusual step of writing a formal contract that she then asked each of the ISD performers to sign. Steve Tavender met with each student individually, went over each point in sequence, then countersigned the contract, keeping one copy for himself and sending one back to Diane. The contract's clauses were as follows, with a space for the student's initials next to each line:

I will be at all rehearsals. (No matter how tired I may feel!)

I will learn my lines by the end of January.

I will be on time. If I am late, I will run laps (first time: one lap for every late minute; second time: two laps for every late minute; third time: three laps, etc.).

I will keep up with my school work.

I will be quiet when I am not on stage.

I will maintain a positive attitude.

I will leave all personal problems outside the theater.

I will focus when I am at rehearsal.

If I break any of the above rules, I understand that I will be replaced, and someone else will play my part on stage.

On balance, the ISD contingent proves the contract to be unnecessary, and Diane later laments not having done something similar for the hearing actors, since it is the Jets who, collectively, are moodier, prone to interrupting, and terminally unfocused. She concludes that deaf teens have attention spans no different from any other teenage group- -the ongoing exception being Joey, who demonstrates a consistent lack of self-control throughout his soon-to-be abbreviated *West Side Story* tenure.

By late March 2000, other defections are also in the air. Pearlene, now addicted to her private pickup rehearsals with Olivia, pushes for Saturday morning rehearsals at ISD. The rest of the Shark girls make it quite clear that they would rather do just about anything else, but Christopher proves responsive, and Diane also agrees to attend, mostly as an extra set of eyes. The time will be spent on perfecting the Shark girls' dance steps, and Diane intends to step in as little as possible. Jen Harris joins up, and spends the time as a bug in Diane's ear, alerting her to translation problems and sloppy signing. As the actors run through their lines, Jen assesses each phrase and then lets Diane know whether they passed muster. Sometimes she just nods her approval, but at other moments, she leans in and whispers, "That sign they're using there won't work," or in more disastrous sections, "Whatever they just signed was nonsense. I am totally confused." When egregious sign mistakes get repeated, Diane sidles over to Christopher—the two of them rarely need an interpreter at this late stage—and asks him, "Is there a way to change this to make it clearer?" Christopher invariably says yes, and works with the students and Jen to find better approaches for the line in question.

One phrase that causes particular trouble comes from "America," where Rosalia (Amy) boasts that she'll buy a big car, and give all of her Puerto Rican cousins a free ride. Anita (Olivia) responds with the acid comment, "How you get all of them inside?" Unfortunately, the word "inside" dangles in space in ASL because it has no referent except back to the previous line, something that no one dealt with when creating the initial translation of the script. Diane and Jen ask Olivia to add the sign for "car" to the end of the line, thus solving the problem—but only after a series of arguments and explanations that takes up ten minutes of valuable rehearsal time and frustrates Jocelyn (as Francisca) in particular, almost to the breaking point. Jocelyn responds with an intentional lethargy, and even Pearlene's entreaties to keep going, to keep getting better, fail to register. Christopher and Diane realize that Jocelyn is fading out, perhaps irreparably, and they begin to wonder about finding a replacement.

I Feel Pretty

When I moved to Springfield, I just thought, "My life as an artist is over." Then you called.

Phil Fiorini

Mid-March 2000. As any theater director will gloomily attest, there comes a time in every rehearsal process where, shortly after the midpoint has been reached, nothing works, nothing can work, and the odds are good that nothing ever will. Morale is low, the set is in a permanent state of half-undress, lighting equipment litters the floor, and tempers flare like geysers. Insignificant misunderstandings become serious grudges; minor irritations turn to festering grievances, each one worn proudly, like a badge. Every adjustment is painful, a bitter pill to swallow. And in *West Side Story*'s case, nobody—nobody at all—is really off book.

The low point turns out to be a long trough in which various participants bottom out one at a time. The problems are exacerbated by an ongoing missing link: an interpreter for Tony. Diane has believed from the first that it is crucial to have a male interpreter to sign the role of Tony, but so far, she has only Andi, Allison, and Anna. Richard Fee, whose department remains terminally short on male students, suggests contacting the Deaf and Hard-of-Hearing Commission in Springfield, headed up by the most powerful Deaf man in the state, Jerry Covell. Without much optimism, Diane tries a cold call and describes the project in some detail to the woman who answers the telephone. "Just a minute," the woman says, "maybe the new guy would be interested. He's an actor or something, hang on."

Enter Phil Fiorini, Jerry Covell's Confidential Assistant and Interpreter. As "an actor or something," Phil has tread various boards, notably in Chicago and New York City, for almost twenty years. Along the way, he has appeared in *West Side Story* no less than three times, in three different roles. He is a somewhat reluctant member of Actors' Equity, but in his own retiring way, he is as proud as a peacock of his status as a nationally certified interpreter. A gentle, slender, sandy-haired man of forty who looks at least five years younger, Phil is the first interpreter the show has seen who not only uses sign language, but naturally and effortlessly emotes as he does so. His actor's training and his ASL studies have reinforced one another to an extraordinary degree; he literally cannot, now, do one without embracing the other. From the moment he joins Ken (as Tony) onstage, it is clear that Phil's presence as a performer will light up the show. As a very well-credentialed interpreter, Phil can clarify the rising pile of manual issues that Andi and Carrie and the ISD students have been unable to solve. He will become what the show has lacked from the start, a sign master.

As a general rule, a sign master takes responsibility for a given work's style and syntax, ironing out discrepancies between different sign languages or sign language users to present a unified approach, a common tongue. The fact that none of the hearing members of the production team ever thought to look for a sign master is ironic, an obvious breakdown of communication; it was assumed by some of the deaf participants and steering committee members that *West Side Story* would require and have a sign master, but that assumption was never passed on. Most members of the hearing production team did not realize that the

Tony sings "Maria" with Phil Fiorini interpreting.

concept of a sign master existed, and consequently saw no need to fill the position.

In practical terms, a sign master can avoid some of the more obvious pitfalls of shortcuts in sign language, especially those that might arise from using Signed English. Using this system, it is possible to take a word like *butterfly* and sign each segment of the word literally, with the first sign signifying *"butter"* and the second, *"fly."* The unintended result: a stick of butter taking flight. ASL avoids such obvious problems by having a specific sign to denote a butterfly, but not everyone in the *West Side Story* cast relies on ASL, and so the word (and song) "Tonight" become problematic, because in Signed English, the word might imply that someone is going directionally toward the night. With Phil on board, logical lapses of this kind are quickly caught and corrected, much to the relief of all concerned.

Unfortunately, Phil's mid-March arrival also shakes up the existing chain of authority. In the beginning, Christopher always took the lead because Diane rightly surmised that the dance sequences would take the longest to learn, and so most of the cast initially fell into believing that the buck stopped with Christopher. Once Diane began work on non-music scenes, she encountered immediate resistance, as if she were throwing her weight around in arbitrary and unacceptable ways. Now Phil, despite working closely with Diane and Christopher, runs into the exact same wall of resentment. Halfway through the first night of his attendance, Diane fields a question of how best to block an interpreted scene, and she turns to Phil, sitting quietly in the back, and demands, "So. Do you want to do this, or not?"

Phil hesitantly stands, and Diane introduces him—but not, unfortunately, to the entire cast, because the scene in question involves only Ken and Pearlene. Phil realizes full well that he's the new kid on the block. He understands what his place, in other circumstances, ought to be. However, he decides that he cannot, in good conscience, allow things to continue as they are. With calm, ineluctable certainty, he informs Diane that the vast majority of the signing currently used by the production's interpreters is improperly staged and illegible. Diane, who wonders why Christopher, dorm parents, or others who've stopped by haven't told her this already, swallows her pride and listens hard. Phil tells her that he is fully aware that time is of the essence, and that only so many changes are possible before opening. Still, he is adamant. As far as he can see, most of the ISD students have not adapted their signing to the requirements of stage work, and he says, quite flatly, that large swaths of the hearing interpreter's work is so garbled that it might as well be a sign system from a completely foreign country.

Diane accepts the majority of his criticisms with good grace and a sinking heart. Together, they draw up plans to rework the placement of the interpreters. Well aware of how the cast will likely react, she then gives Phil almost free reign to correct, cajole, and belabor both the Sharks and the hearing interpreters into correct sign usage and grammar. Phil patiently works through each scene as it comes up on the schedule, solving one problem at a time. He is deferential, soft-spoken but firm; it is quite clear that he expects his pointers to be taken as orders, not suggestions. The cast, quietly, rumbles and fumes. To many, he remains an interloper—and interlopers are not made welcome in the tiny, emotionally cramped spaces of theater productions. Who, they wonder, is this new face, and why is he the one suddenly giving orders?

Gus Stewart, a friend of Christopher's and a colleague of Phil's, manages to make matters worse. On Phil's third night at rehearsal, Gus asks to come along and then, while watching a hallway rehearsal with the Jets and the Sharks, proceeds to not only make suggestions, but to make them directly to the actors. Gus's interference makes it suddenly permissible for everyone to add his or her two cents worth, and directing by committee becomes the word of the day. No one reacts well to this, and because it was Phil who drove Gus in from Springfield, it is Phil who bears the brunt of the cast's objections, their surly blame. The Jets, especially, tighten up, behaving exactly like the insular gang they're supposed to portray. Phil, for them, becomes a nonentity at best, an enemy at worst.

Diane and Phil, however, are busy with Pearlene Jo and Ken inside the actual theater space, and neither realizes what Gus's interference has done—or that it even happened—until after the rehearsal. The next day, Phil calls Diane and they voice their mutual displeasure at Gus's well-intentioned but hands-on approach. They agree that Gus may come back if he wishes, but only with explicit instructions that any further advice must be routed through Christopher, Diane, or Terri. That night, Gus watches calmly from the audience and says not a word. He never says precisely why, but he does not make another appearance, except to see one of the final performances.

Ironically, Gus had been Diane's initial choice to play Glad Hand. He had contacted ISD in February 2000 and asked about appearing in the show. Diane, in turn, asked Christopher about Gus and received a glowing report. One day later, Gus informed Diane in a follow-up e-mail that he had a sudden transportation problem. A highway patrolman had pulled him over for speeding the night before, and in the process, the officer discovered that Gus had not renewed his vehicle registration. The officer proceeded to suspend Gus's license, leaving Gus with no way to reach Jacksonville for rehearsals. Unable to discover a solution, Diane and Gus mutually agreed that he would not be able to take the role—although Diane continued to hold out a secret hope that Gus might be able to resolve his license issues quickly and still become her Glad Hand. At this late date, however, Glad Hand's shoes have been filled by Christopher, and so for the second time, Gus is suddenly out of the picture.

Luckily, two people take to Phil immediately, the first being Christopher and the second, Andi Kreps. Christopher sees in Phil a helpmeet and a sympathetic ear, exactly the sort of assistant the show has needed. Christopher's own energies have been taken up entirely by the dance routines—and now, by Glad Hand—and he has not had the time or mental reserves to spare on issues of clarity or Deaf communication. It becomes a familiar sight to find Christopher and Phil talking in the parking lot, often across the hood of Christopher's newly acquired copper-brown Oldsmobile, well after rehearsals are over and the building is locked tight. For her part, Andi's dearest wish has finally been granted, to defer her leadership role to a truly experienced interpreter. As soon as she sees him interpreting, she thinks, "Thank God he's here," and not only does she allow him to assume authority, she practically throws it at him. Phil, in turn, realizes Andi is his best lieutenant and sets about restoring that authority as quickly as she'll allow, telling Anna and Allison to look to Andi for help and assistance. It takes time, but the ploy works. Slowly, with the obvious support of Andi, Christopher, and Diane, the rest of the cast comes to accept Phil and his last-minute meddling.

Nowhere is this meddling more helpful than in "I Feel Pretty," the show's resident albatross. It refuses to come to life and weighs on the second act like an anchor. Phil's solution is quick, simple, and painless. He installs Jen Harris as a mirror (Jen provides a voice for Shark girl Francisca during the scene), and has her sit in the shadow of Terri's piano. From there, Jen, who can hear every note, signs the lyrics of the song back to Pearlene and her girlfriends, keeping them at once on the beat and also on the correct lines. The change makes theatrical, if not logical, sense, since the libretto calls for an actual mirror, and to substitute a flesh-and-blood actor for the mirror pushes a literal reference into the realm of the metaphor. The salient point: it works. With Jen safely perched on one of the set's ubiquitous milk crates, she can only be seen by a select few members of the audience; the rest will believe, as they should, that Pearlene and company are flying through the song entirely on their own. For the first time, Pearlene can concentrate on the movements and the blocking, because she no longer has to worry about keeping herself tethered to a beat she cannot feel. Jen, however, intent on signing cues, begins to lose track of the harmonies she's supposed to be singing. In the course of hiding the Jen-as-mirror from the audience, Jen has become separated by the length of Terri's piano from her fellow choristers, Helen Brattain and Anna Poplett. Not only can Jen not see Helen and Anna, but she has no time to make proper eye contact even if she could. Phil solves this new problem by moving Jen back to her original position and performing the part of the mirror himself. Everything else follows in due course, and although "I Feel Pretty" never manages to really rocket off the stage, it does achieve a life of its own—a life born in a looking glass.

Phil also rearranges the blocking within established scenes. In the process, he brings to the table a new term for theatrical interpretation, "zoning." Zoning involves the placement of interpreters in different areas of the stage so that actors moving across the space are never far from an available translator. In contrast with platform, stationary, or shadow interpreting, zoning allows different interpreters to pick up a given actor's dialogue depending on where they are onstage. For example, if Anybodys begins a scene stage left and then gravitates to stage right, her lines would be interpreted first by the interpreter in Zone 1, then by the interpreter in Zone 2 (see below).

Zone 2 ◄——————— **Anybodys   Zone 1**

In theory, an unlimited number of zones may be created on the stage, for as many crosses, moves, or actions as might be required. The reality is somewhat different, if only because of space restrictions and sight lines. A zone that can't be seen is useless, and Phil becomes the latest production member to bemoan the limits imposed by enclosing such a large cast in such a small space. Yet, the small space provides advantages in that no actor absolutely must be switched over from one interpreter to another within a scene. The farthest an actor can possibly get from an interpreter is a distance of thirty feet, and in scenes where this occurs, the interpreter, by shadowing, can follow.

Based largely on the number of people onstage, *West Side Story* eventually adopts all four basic interpretive styles, one tumbling after the next like dice. For a pre-show announcement ("No smoking, no flash photography, the fire exit is behind the third scaffold from the right"), Becky Cline provides platform interpreting. Then, when the show begins, the interpreters abandon the stage and the actors perform "The Prologue" without speech of any kind—until Schrank and Krupke arrive. This brings out Andi, Anna, and Allison. They take their position and hold it because the action that follows is largely center stage. Tony's first scenes (especially the song, "Something's Coming") eschew the stationary style in favor of shadowed interpretation. Zoning makes a rare appearance in the first of Maria's bridal shop scenes, and then dissolves back to a modified blend of shadow and zone as the scene segues directly into the capacity crowd of "Dance at the Gym." Phil assures Diane that although the audience will be hard-pressed to follow every last detail, it will only be worse if the interpreting doesn't match the needs of the scene. He believes that what the interpreters must do is "find the builds in the scenes and *hit* them!" This is actor-speak, familiar territory for Diane, as relaxing for her as a good massage. She puts her energies back into tweaking the blocking and acting—especially Pearlene's—and lets Phil place the interpreters as the builds demand.

The blocking in the Jets' scenes requires the most readjustment, because prior to Phil's arrival, the interpreters had been stowed away on top of various scaffolds, especially the one that looms directly over Doc's shop. This gave the Jets complete freedom to roam the stage and ensured there would be no sight line problems. In Phil's brave new world, the interpreters join their Jet counterparts at ground level. Not only does the stage space become more crowded, but the Jets have to watch where they step or risk blocking an interpreter. Once again, the Jets close ranks and pout. Once more, Diane finds herself prying their good humor free as if they were oysters, not actors. It doesn't help matters that she has a second request, not just of the Jets, but of the cast in general. In order not to shift focus unnecessarily away from the interpreters, she tells everyone, "Stop fidgeting. Remain alive onstage, but—keep your movements controlled."

In an all-hearing production, only the most unmotivated or excessive motions would need to be tamped down, but in *West Side Story,* with the deaf audience tracking back and forth

Tony and Doc (Jay Peterson) weigh their options in the basement of Doc's soda shop. Sign interpreters Phil Fiorini and Andi Kreps stand below.

between performers and interpreters, it is essential that they not be cued accidentally or drawn to look in places where nothing of any import is happening. To achieve this, the interpreters have to relearn their roles. Diane, assuming that interpreting would be much like other acting, had asked her interpreting crew to be just as animated as the actors they signed for, but Phil suggests that this is too much, that the visual cues for the deaf (and possibly hearing) audience would be lost in the shuffle. Instead, he suggests that the interpreters come alive in spurts, as their lines come up. Thus, if all three female interpreters are onstage and Anna has a line to interpret, the other two interpreters turn their attention to her, as if she's just caught the only available playground ball. Rather than staying in character themselves, it becomes their job to make Anna the focus of the moment. Only when all three sign together, as they do for "Gee, Officer

Krupke," do they have the luxury of remaining live the entire time. The trick, as Phil explains, is to avoid complete lapses into stasis during quieter moments, or in between lines. "Seize the focus," he tells Andi, "and then, give it back."

Phil quickly realizes which sections will require the least reorganization: any sequence where the two rival gangs speak to each other (and to no one else). As Diane writes:

> Given the story we were trying to tell—the Jets and the Sharks fight because they do not speak the same language—we put the actors and the audience in the very situation that precipitated their rivalry. We took away all the standard tools of communication for each side and made the deaf actors stop signing while the hearing actors turned their voices off. As a result, they had to do what deaf and hearing people would do if faced with each other in their everyday lives: they gestured to each other using a crude form of PSE. The trick was for the actors to make their gestures specific and clear enough so that the audience could understand the flow of the lines in the same way that they would if they were hearing or seeing the written text of the scene.[1]

In this, it is clear to Phil that Diane has succeeded. The gangs struggle through their encounters and drag the audience along with them. Leaving them to their own devices is both realistic and compelling, and to plaster interpreters over the top of the action would be a mistake both logically and dramatically—and Phil wisely chooses to spend his energies elsewhere.

It takes a week, but Pearlene finally can't contain herself any longer. During a break while working on "Somewhere" with Phil, she suddenly stamps her foot to get his attention, wrinkles up her nose in a definitive scowl, and demands he explain how he knows "the language"—ASL—better than she does. "You're not even Deaf!" she exclaims.

Phil suspects she will not appreciate the answer, but he replies anyway, telling her, "I went to school and trained for this. I've taken classes. For years."

Pearlene has not had the same opportunity. Despite her status as a native speaker of ASL, despite being born into a Deaf family who support the idea of Deaf culture, her schooling has not given her formal training in ASL. Like most schools for the deaf, ISD does not offer classes in ASL. It is taught, but only through osmosis, by teachers and administrators who use it, and from the students themselves, who pass the knowledge from one to another just as they would anything else, through conversation. ASL is not, however, an academic pursuit, as Spanish or Russian might be in a mainstream, hearing school. The closest equivalent would be studies in Deaf history and culture, classes that cover famous deaf figures, many American, and the development of Deaf social and political climates. Some argue that leaving ASL out of the curriculum is the equivalent of not teaching English grammar as a separate course in a "normal" school, whereas others insist that there are other, more important subjects to cover and only so much time in the day. Opponents feel that ASL can be picked up, learned and mastered at any time by anyone with sufficient interest; it has no more business appearing in a lesson plan than does Australian poetry or the correct manufacture of a birch bark canoe.

Phil began his training late in life, in 1990, during a break from acting. He moved from Chicago back to Kansas City and studied to become a certified interpreter in Kansas. His motivations were legion, but heading up the list was a desire to move to New York City, try his luck as an actor, and *not* to wait tables. His plan worked. New York State honored his Kansas certification, and he was able to pay the rent and cover his bills with freelance interpreting jobs while still finding time to pursue an acting career that took him as far as Off-Broadway (*Thanatos*) and a traveling company performing both *Greater Tuna* and *A Tuna*

Christmas. Between shows, he found time to become certified at the national level. Like the Illinois-based ISAS, the test involves a written portion and, more crucially, a manual test where the applicant must react to and interpret deaf speakers on a filmstrip or video. Phil, in retrospect, feels the test is highly subjective, because it is possible to give an entire range of correct answers for much of what is said. It is, he feels, an ongoing problem within Deaf culture, in that their interpreters are not—and never can be—of equal quality, from one to the next. The fact that most states have their own in-house standards and testing systems makes it possible to become a certified interpreter but lack important skills that a neighboring state might well demand.

Phil himself admits to having a gift, but reserves true black-belt status to native ASL signers, meaning those who are born deaf and into a Deaf family—and who've had more practice than Pearlene. What he will claim for himself is a certain correctness. He makes a special point of signing with great precision, of not varying from accepted syntax or dropping into local slang unless he specifically intends to do so.

Phil, unsurprisingly, views acting and interpreting as a natural mix, the one fortifying the other not only through experience (interpreting theater performances, for example, something he has done for years) but also through their innate similarity. Both are essentially forms of communication, a particular species of translation. Both are inherently physical. Both improve when invested with emotion. Basic interpreting, as Phil sees it, is not difficult, but he believes many interpreters "speak the language but never sing." Phil sets out to raise *West Side Story*'s interpreters to the level of soloists. He insists that facial expression and beautiful gestures are not sufficient. Phil wants the interpreters to incorporate ASL poetry.

If such an inclusion of poetry and poetic expression ever became part of the criterion for full-blown language status, ASL could immediately relax its ongoing fight for recognition as one of the world's legitimate systems. Poetry, however, tends to be associated with the written word and the process of longhand composition, and because ASL poetry is virtually unknown to the non-Deaf world, this impression is not likely to change. Unlike written poetry, the kind that appears in a chapbook and is marketed on bookshelves, ASL poetry is manual in form. In order to "read" it, one must attend in person and view the poet at work, or as a distant second, watch the performance on tape. An exact definition of ASL poetry is probably outside the purview of written English. Like Justice Rehnquist's famous definition of pornography, "we know it when we see it"—but, like the tree falling in the forest, if no one is present to view ASL poetry, it simply didn't happen.

Descriptive examples, however, abound. Phil demonstrates one possibility by taking a typically cloying staple of written English poetry—a single leaf falling from a tree—and describing the event through sign. He begins by mimicking the leaf as it falls, using his down-turned palm to imitate the fluttering wind-borne leaf as it wafts back and forth, much in the same manner as a child might affect the same demonstration. Over top of this basic rubric, Phil then adds the ASL signs for LEAF, LONELINESS, and FALLING, capping it all with a lyrical fingerspelled version of the action. To apply this to *West Side Story*, consider the moment when Tony begins the song "Maria"; he is full to the brim with longing and a sudden fascination with the very syllables of Maria's name. Phil enacts both the words and Tony's passion by making the ASL sign for GOOSE BUMPS, then fingerspelling Maria's name up his shivering arm. The effect is beautiful, not only to ASL speakers but also to those who cannot fully comprehend what he's done. The poetry of it shines through regardless.

Although Phil works regularly—even constantly—with the *West Side Story* interpreters, he steers clear of assisting the ISD high schoolers except to correct what he feels might be egregious mistakes. Their translations, their specific signs, have already been set in stone, and he deems it foolish, even dangerous, to alter them. In literal terms, for example, the sign that the ISD students have arrived at for Puerto Rican is, essentially, the letters *P* and *R*, with a specific gangland flourish for added effect. (Richard, as Schrank, translates both "PRs" and "spic"—sometimes unsuccessfully, in Phil's estimation—to "NIGGER," the most offensive and derogatory statement he can think of.) The sign for the Sharks, accomplished every time with a single hand, translates to a nonsense sound, akin to the letters Q and K being jammed together. The sign for the Jets is clear at least in its derivative sense, in that it's been built as a variation on the sign for a downward flying airplane, but the end result is suspiciously close to "I love you," instead. Intent on honoring the work that has already been done, Phil makes a pact with himself to leave the Sharks and their syntax alone. Instead, he goes after the interpreters—and, on occasion, Pearlene. Gradually, the mood of the cast lightens. Some even begin to feel a certain optimism, as if the bottom at last has been reached They are wrong. The bottom is just around the corner.

Somewhere

The world's a theatre, the earth a stage,

Which God and Nature do with actors fill.

Thomas Heywood
Apology for Actors, 1612

On March 27, Joey Gillis (Chino) fails to board the ISD bus at the end of the school's spring break and, in so doing, effectively becomes the eighth actor to quit the faltering cast. In much of the world, missing a bus would be a minor incident, no cause for alarm. ISD, however, has a very strict policy regarding the transport of its student body: Either a student arrives at campus on the ISD bus or they must be returned to school by a parent or legal guardian. A student cannot simply return of his or her own accord, nor are students allowed to catch another bus, even if one were available. Greyhound does not service Jacksonville. Neither does Trailways or any other regular bus line; the nearest bus stops are in Springfield, as is the Amtrak line. Thus, by virtue of missing the bus, Joey has, de facto, withdrawn himself from school. Indefinitely.

Rumors abound, headed up by a consensus opinion from the remainder of the ISD cast that Joey has stayed behind to "hang out with friends." No one seems surprised, least of all Pearlene, who erroneously warned Diane via e-mail in early

January that Joey had already flown the coop. "He is not here anymore," she wrote. "He've been gone for a long time. I don't think he'll be here anytime soon or later! So find a replacement."

By the time of Monday night's rehearsal, efforts to contact Joey and his family have failed and, once again, *West Side Story* faces a crisis. The role of Chino, although limited, is key to the dramatic movement of the plot. It is Chino who, despondent at Bernardo's death and betrayed by Maria, obtains a gun and shoots Tony. Without Chino, the story lacks the man who is arguably its most dramatic agent. Furthermore, Chino's character has been fully integrated into the Shark gang, and thus anyone stepping into the role will have to learn the choreography behind at least four major dance sequences. The obvious choice—fire and replace Joey immediately—thus appears anything but obvious. Diane concedes that waiting will likely only prolong the agony, but with precious few other prospects, she is tempted. Hoping for Joey's return also holds drawbacks, because with opening night only two weeks away, even a single day away from the production will seriously hamper Joey's performance.

This is not a new situation for Diane. In each of her four previous Mac productions, she has lost one or more actors. Sometimes she blames herself, but mostly she faults what many see as a regional and possibly generational trend toward a lack of follow-through and personal responsibility. With many Mac students, a word given is not a word kept. The notion that action and commitments come burdened with consequences does not appear to occur to many of the college's students. Dropping out of a theater production—which, along with team sports, is the ultimate in collegiate cooperative endeavors—not only leaves a director high and dry, it risks upending the whole apple-cart. Diane has pulled off some very fly-by-night recruiting, often by stopping students in lunch lines, accosting them between classes, and chasing them down on the sidewalks. She has a knack for fast-talking near-strangers into joining a suddenly bereft production. More often than not, she has succeeded, and all of her productions have—so far—come off in the end. It is a standing joke among the faculty and administration that it's best to avoid Diane when she's in rehearsal. If you don't, you risk being cast, whether you like it or not.

Finding a replacement for Joey presents a special challenge. Never before has anyone dropped out (or vanished) with so little time left in the rehearsal process. Nor will just any Mac student do because the person chosen *has to be deaf.* If he isn't, the entire house of cards on which the casting has been based will completely fall apart. The only apparent option is to pull one of the Sharks from the general pool, even if it throws off the numerical détente currently enjoyed between the two gangs. Diane quickly settles on Michael Nesmith, currently playing Louis, and she expects to make the announcement of Michael's nominal promotion first thing at Monday night's rehearsal. But, on Monday night, fate disguised as bad planning once again intervenes. Michael does not show up. The other ISD students report that he is skipping rehearsal in favor of a track meet and will not be back until the next day. Stunned, Diane does the only thing she feels she can still reasonably do. She plucks Christopher Smith out of the audience, strips him of the role of Glad Hand, and turns him, with a wave of her directorial wand, into Chino.

In the moment that this happens, no one realizes how this one simple act will effectively remove Christopher from the collaborative process. Glad Hand appears onstage only once, briefly, but Chino weaves through scene after scene. So, although Christopher remains on the set, the geographical shift from watching in the audience to performing on the stage cuts the ties that bind him to Diane and Terri. Almost instantaneously, he disappears as a member of the production's ruling junta and steps into the role of a full-time cast member, with all the attendant duties of the latter, and a great deal of catching up to do.

(Christopher, remembering the switch later, said, "I had to adjust the character from Glad Hand to Chino, it is like changing from colorful to tragic.") Although he does continue to work with the ISD students on off days (at ISD), and despite his best efforts to "stay flexible whatever the situations pop up," he never again has the freedom to step into a dance and improve, tweak, or redirect it; he never again finds himself able to simply sit back and evaluate the action onstage.

Christopher's "promotion" leaves Michael Nesmith both furious and hurt. From the beginning, Michael has wanted a larger role than the one he's been handed, and he seems to believe that he deserves it, a priori. He certainly comes equipped with a fine glower and more than his share of teenage sulk, but like many young actors, he finds it difficult to focus himself when he has nothing specific to do onstage. This makes it tricky for Diane to judge his overall talent level. Still, she has already opted to expand his role in the production by giving him the starring part in the ballet duet of "Somewhere," which Michael dances with Dawn Williams. He works diligently on the steps and the timing, with the surprising result—apparent even before dress rehearsals—that the ballet becomes one of the show's most touching and emotional moments. The ballet, however, is a non-speaking part, and Michael, as a Shark, still does not have a single official line. Lines are what he craves, and when he discovers, the next day, that he has missed the opportunity of playing Chino, who is second only to Bernardo among the Sharks for sheer volume of spoken (or signed) lines, he is visibly upset. He pleads his case to Diane, telling her that his track coach ordered him to attend the meet, even though the coach in question knew full well that Michael had made a commitment to *West Side Story* and couldn't go to meets on nights when he had rehearsals.

Diane, in the midst of scooting actors into their places for the first scene of the night, does her best to listen and apologize all in one breath, but the single salient fact—that the decision has already been made—is not something Michael is ready to hear. He tries twice more that night to convince her, and with each successive failure, his mood darkens. The rehearsal moves on without him—or, without him as Chino. Once, after Diane gives him a specific direction in a crowd scene, Michael gives her the finger from behind another actor's back. Diane, already intent on another fix, does not see the gesture. Christopher does but he chooses not to mention it. Michael's blue funk lasts well into the next week and his acting suffers for it. He concentrates only during his star turn in the ballet, a job that he continues to take extremely seriously. The rest of the time, he looks as if he'd much rather be cruising the mall.

With Christopher now ensconced as Chino, the show suddenly lacks—again—a Glad Hand. On the advice of Chuck Nash, Diane contacts April Garvey, a high school junior at ISD who, so far, has not expressed any particular interest in the show. April agrees to attend a rehearsal and "check things out." It is obvious from the first that she has a flair and vitality that would make her perfect not just for Glad Hand, a sad-sack sort of role, but for one of the Shark girls. Leaving her as Glad Hand and only Glad Hand would clearly be a terrible waste of her energetic, natural stage presence. Christopher and Diane convince her to take not only Glad Hand but also Francisca. Like Christopher, April has a tremendous amount of catch-up work to do. She will have to learn not only the lines and blocking for Glad Hand's one and only scene ("Dance at the Gym"), but she'll have to figure out the footwork for two involved dances besides.

April's presence alleviates the sudden loss of Jocelyn Cleary, the previous incarnation of Francisca. The role of Francisca, like all of the Shark girlfriends, is not especially crucial to the dramatic engines of the plot, but not having Jocelyn, who had been with the show from the beginning, critically impairs the Shark girls' two principal numbers, "America" and "I Feel Pretty." On the last day that she attends rehearsal, Jocelyn refuses to rise from her seat in the audience. Huffy orders from Pearlene and others have no effect. When Diane approaches Jocelyn and asks, through an interpreter, why she won't move, Jocelyn just shrugs. Every ounce of her body language tells the world that she is through rehearsing, that she knows her part as well as anyone needs to know it, and no power on earth can move her one inch closer to the stage. Diane does her best to hide from the rest of the cast how much this fruitless exchange upsets her, and she proceeds to work the scenes without Jocelyn for the remainder of the night. Early next morning, she calls Steve Tavender and explains the situation. Steve brings Jocelyn into his office and tries semi-successfully to plumb the depths of Jocelyn's mind-set. When, despite this discussion, Jocelyn refuses to promise that she will behave better in future, he accedes to Diane's request and fires her.

Seven days later, Jocelyn's mother calls Diane's office number, ready to purchase tickets to the show for family members. She has no idea that Jocelyn has been let go, and Diane, expecting an ugly confrontation, does her best to let her down gently. To her surprise, Jocelyn's mother takes the news in stride. "Was it her attitude?" she asks, a question to which Diane cautiously answers in the affirmative. "I thought so," replies Jocelyn's mother. "I'm sorry she let you down."

Gee, Officer Krupke

My favorite part of the show was "Officer Krupke," because it is so full of theatrical, visualize, and accessibles (shadowed interpreters involved). Plus, my other favorites were "Somewhere" and the last scene of Maria holds the gun when she outbursted . . . just because it impacted me that they are telling a story to change the world for the better and life it soo short if the world won't change it.

Christopher Smith
E-mail, 5/5/00

West Side Story contains two traditional showstoppers. The first is "America," which comes midway through the first act. The second is "Gee, Officer Krupke," a song that positively bubbles with energy. Its inclusion in the second act is due entirely to the "drunken porter" defense used by Arthur Laurents, who battled tirelessly to keep "Krupke" where it is. The rest of the production team wanted to bump it to the first act, where its basic lightheartedness made more logical sense. As Sondheim remembered,

> Here is a group of kids running from a double murder, and for them to stop and do this comic number seemed to me to be out of place. I kept nudging Arthur and Jerry to reverse the two. We didn't, and of course "Krupke" works wonderfully in the second act . . . there was theatrical truth in putting "Krupke" there, if not literal truth.[1]

Laurents's "drunken porter" argument hails back to Shakespeare and the scene in the so-called "Scottish play"—in theater circles, superstition holds that to say the play's real name, *MacBeth*, is a surefire recipe for disaster—where, with the tragedy and bloodshed well under way, the action screams to a stop as a plastered night watchman bumbles around the stage, trying to open the keep's main door. Comedy, argued Laurents, is exactly what's needed in the face of tragedy; it's the tension between the two that holds the audience. Curiously, in the film version, "Cool" and "Krupke" were reversed, just as Sondheim had suggested. Consequently, "Cool" gains in effect, depicting the helplessness of the Jets, their taut-as-a-wire tension after Riff's death, but "Krupke" suffers. It comes too early, and its clowning, although amusing to the audience, is no longer cathartic or dramatically necessary to the Jets themselves.

Mac's version of "Krupke" shouldn't work no matter where it appears in the script, which calls for no less than eight Jets (including "Acemen, Rocketmen, Rank and File," the script's own delineation of the Jet hierarchy ranging from Riff down to Baby John). Diane has only four available Jets, because Riff is long since dead by the time this number comes up, and Anybodys is not yet an accepted member of the gang. Gaps appear in the lyrics, lines must be covered, parts are paved over or doubled. But thanks to an exuberant performance, Richard Atkins (Action), Dane Vincent (Diesel), Prentice Southwell (A-Rab), and Bryce Hoffman (Baby John) very nearly steal the show.

None of the four is in any way connected to ISD. None of the four attended the November auditions. Only one of the four (Dane) even attended the first night of rehearsals—an event which became his audition. ("So," he was asked afterward, "did Terri say you can sing?") Stranger still, three of the four have nothing to do with Mac. Bryce is the lone Mac representative, a freshman who made the mistake of walking past Diane's office on a day when she was down to just a single male Jet. As it turned

The Jets sing "Gee, Officer Krupke."

out, Bryce was on his way to visit Meredith, and he soon found himself belabored into the role. As Baby John, Bryce has exactly the right blend of bald-faced shock and potentially violent innocence. As an actor, he has the furthest distance to travel, despite the fact that he has already appeared in a high school production of *West Side Story*. Luckily for everyone involved, Bryce has a solid work ethic, and he regularly stays late to ask questions about his character and to perfect his dance steps. The dancing, however, comes hard; his feet refuse to go where he tells them. However, by the end of the process, Diane and his three compatriot Jets, together with Riff and Anybodys, have transported him to heights that no one expected he could achieve. If it's true that imitation is the sincerest form of flattery, then the other three Jets should feel justly complimented; whatever energy and spirit Bryce summons can be traced directly to Bryce's own diligence and the relative wealth of stage experience and genuine talent exhibited by Richard, Dane, and Prentice.

Prentice Southwell, from day one, becomes the show's resident "character." His name comes up through the Jacksonville Theater Guild, and Diane's contacts there warn her that Prentice lives and works in Beardstown, forty-five minutes north of Jacksonville. Diane calls anyway, and Prentice immediately agrees to audition. At twenty-nine, he's developed a receding hairline, a "problem" Jen Harris quickly covers with a dark blue winter hat to keep the audience from noticing his age. He makes his living, at least at the outset, as a church youth leader. On weekends, he attends revivals and spreads the gospel. He announces, one evening just before rehearsal, that the previous weekend was a particular success. "We saved thirty souls," he proclaims, "and we got something like twenty kids to sign their vows of abstinence."

Prentice never lacks for words. He talks and mutters almost constantly, whether anyone listens or not. He is funny, clever, and unguarded; it is common for Prentice to enter someone else's conversation, quite unannounced, or to carry on one of his own, making comments and observations in a steadily falling cadence. Carrie Moore, frustrated at his frequent interruptions, resorts to bringing a roll of duct tape to rehearsals. She warns others that every time Prentice opens his mouth, she's going to pull a section of the tape. If she gets a long enough strip, she'll tear it off and wrap it around his head.

Late in the rehearsal process, Prentice switches jobs and begins work at a grocery store, but this doesn't last long. By the time *West Side Story* closes, Prentice is unemployed and talking about leads instead of souls. "I've got an in," he says, nodding confidently, as if it's already a done deal. "Plus, I won't have to work weekends, and I'll actually get a chance to see my wife!"

Heather Southwell, Prentice's wife, eventually takes over as *West Side Story*'s box office manager. She tells the production team, "We knew we had to be involved in this show as soon as we heard about it." Prentice's sister, who was deaf, had died the year before, and her favorite show had always been *West Side Story*.

For Prentice, his daily ninety-mile commute is a pilgrimage made in her honor.

Richard Atkins, bony and rail-thin, with a cowlick of deep brown hair, knew Diane slightly even before the production, because Diane had tried to recruit Richard, a recent graduate of Jacksonville High School, for the fall production of *Ghosts*. A member of the Church of Jesus Christ of Latter-day Saints (also known as the Mormon Church), Richard wound up spending the fall semester at Brigham Young University, but he only attended for a single semester. He has returned to Jacksonville to prepare for his upcoming mission, and works evening shifts at Bound-To-Stay-Bound Books, a successful local bindery. When Diane calls him about doing *West Side Story*, he expresses interest but has to make certain he can switch his work schedule. The bindery is accommodating, but not immediately; as a result, Richard misses an entire week of rehearsals and all of Christopher's incipient choreography. None of the Jets has more catch-up to do in the dance department than Richard, but luckily, none proves to be a quicker study.

Dane Vincent has chosen not to "go the college route," at least for now. He works the graveyard shift at the Amerihost Inn, one of the half dozen motels littering the fast-food strip of Morton Avenue. Thanks to conflicts at home, Dane also lives at the Amerihost, in room 208, one of a series of rooms damaged when a tipsy guest applied his cigarette lighter to a sprinkler head, causing an entire wing's worth of sprinklers to activate. If the Amerihost had a restaurant, Dane could conceivably live out his entire life inside his place of work. The lobby around the front desk has a television, usually tuned to the Weather Channel, and endless supplies of coffee and orange juice. It does not, however, resemble a home. If it weren't for the fact that the lobby looks out directly onto a trim indoor swimming pool, it could easily be mistaken for a nurse's station at a hospital.

The nocturnal environment of the Amerihost is one that Dane has come to loathe, but, so far, he has been unable to switch into daytime work. Whereas the rest of the cast ends their day with *West Side Story*, Dane's day is just beginning. He gets up at four in the afternoon, eats breakfast—one Rally's hamburger, fries, and a Coke—and heads for rehearsal. Dane, who is constantly in motion, is not a small person. On opening night, he stands six foot one and weighs 308 pounds, making him one of the largest Jets ever. Luckily, his dominating presence fits Diesel perfectly. When he appears at the rumble, ready to fight Bernardo, everyone in the audience can feel his bulk as something dangerous, physical, and downright overwhelming. Despite his evident bravado, CJ's waif-like Bernardo hasn't got a prayer against Dane.

Dane's most difficult opponent turns out to be himself. By his own admission, he is a person for whom change is difficult, inherently threatening. Although he professes an undying love of spontaneity, he has a permanent fear of chaos and has dedicated a great deal of time and energy to staving off the unpredictable. His first defense is the safety of routines. His "morning" ritual (rising at a certain time, the Rally's breakfast) is only the tip of the iceberg. He proceeds to arrive at rehearsals before anyone else, often an hour early, which gives him a chance to "absorb the atmosphere" and decompress with the help of a belt-mounted CD player and four CDs—the same four CDs, week after week after week. He begins with heavy current rock, Korn and Limp Bizkit, and ends with either *Phantom of the Opera* or Fleetwood Mac. Dane claims to be heavily influenced by Fleetwood Mac—Stevie Nicks in particular—together with various Eastern philosophies, a casserole of Buddhism, Taoism, and Confucianism. His favorite book is Sun Tzu's *The Art of War*, a tome that he sees as a primer for dealing with hostility, both the world's and his own. It doesn't always help. When taking trips to the big city—Springfield—Dane drives only as far as the White Oaks Mall. The mall is familiar, safe; anywhere else is too jarring, devoid of the safety of routine. If he has to go somewhere past the mall, then someone else must drive.

Unfortunately for Dane, *West Side Story* is one long process of tinkering and trimming, amendment piling on amendment until, at the final gun, most of the initial stage and dance directions have become as extinct as the dinosaurs. This is often not the way of high school or local community theaters, and it is in those arenas that Dane has had his most recent and influential stage experience. (He describes the director of his last production, *Joseph and the Amazing Technicolor Dreamcoat*, as "a profound individual" and "a force to be reckoned with.") Dane is accustomed to blocking a scene, rehearsing it as needed, and locking it into place. Changes are rare, momentous occasions. For Diane—and for Christopher, who constantly updates and fiddles with his choreography—change is the essential form of theater. The clash of styles and personalities is inevitable.

The difficulties begin with Dane's assigned role, a combination of Diesel and Big Deal. Diesel is the sticking point because Diesel, as the script makes perfectly clear, is not the brightest light in the universe. In fact, he's stupid. Dane accepts the role, but also takes offense; why, he wonders, should he have to play the big, dumb fat guy? Why, for that matter, wasn't he cast as Tony? Like Meredith before him, he worries that he's been typecast to the point that he will be unable to rise above the restrictions of the role. Diane, well aware that Dane would prefer to be virtually any other Jet—especially Action—tries to mollify him by getting him to treat the role as a challenge. How, she asks, can he breathe life into Diesel without reducing him to a stereotype? Dane responds with a slow-burn pout that builds and builds. As rehearsals wear on and key roles remain unfilled, Dane's frustration grows. He wonders how he can be expected to interact with a Doc who isn't present—and how can he learn his blocking if there's no Tony to work with?

Even when the casting solidifies, Dane keeps finding himself at the center of changes. When Joey abdicates the role of Chino, all the careful work in "The Rumble" goes by the wayside, and suddenly he and Christopher have to switch positions as teacher and student. By chance more than design, Chino and Diesel are frequent (if antagonistic) dance partners throughout the show, and so it falls to Dane to teach Christopher the steps, the moves required. Even though Christopher has invented the dances— "The Prologue," "Dance at the Gym," "The Rumble"—he has never had to repeat them to the point of perfection. Dane is suddenly the resident expert, and he and Christopher begin working through each step before rehearsals, covering each dance while dodging Carrie Moore's broom ("If I never have to sweep another floor in my life, I'll die happy."). The extra work pays off quickly, aided by the fact that Dane knows fingerspelling. He has also picked up more than his share of signs from the ISD students. Christopher, unsurprisingly, proves to be a quick study, and in no time, Dane has the pleasure of beating Christopher's head, not Joey's, into a pulp against the scaffolds.

Dane's distrust of his director remains intact, and he continues to be one of Diane's most difficult, recalcitrant actors. The least adjustment or request sends Dane into an immediate funk, one which threatens, time and time again, to take the rest of the Jets down with it. With Joey's departure, followed so quickly by Jocelyn's, Dane nearly throws in the towel himself.

Two people stand in his way. The first is Nathan Grieme, the assistant stage manager. Nathan realizes that Dane is about to burst and, unbeknownst to anyone on the creative team, gently talks him down and coaxes him back onto the stage. Dane's mother finishes Nathan's work when Dane, in a phone call home, explains that he "just can't take it anymore." His life outside the theater is not what he would like, and inside the theater, the repetition of the dances has grated to the bone (if one person makes a mistake, Diane insists that everyone do it over). Dane hopes to receive his mother's blessing, or at least her tacit support, but instead she chews him out.

"Dante Vincent," she fumes, using his full name for emphasis (she named him after Dante Alighieri), "I raised you better than that. This lady gave you a chance, and she's got a plan. She called you and you agreed, and you're going to see this thing through. You will tough it out—and you will keep your big mouth shut!"

Like a page torn from Arthur Laurents's other monster hit, *Gypsy*, Dane finds himself stage-mothered back into the play. He makes no attempt to call his father, knowing already his father's opinion of music and theater. "He thinks it's gay," Dane explains. "We don't talk anymore."

Family or no family, the eventual cure turns out to be the sudden, somewhat surprising success of the dress rehearsals. After a painful four-hour cue-to-cue (a technical rehearsal that integrates, usually for the first time, the sound and lighting cues with the actor's entrances, exits, and dialogue), no one has very high expectations for the show in general. In retrospect, this pessimism was largely unfounded; had anyone counted, they would have realized that the cue-to-cue involved over ninety lighting cues, and to finish in anything under eight hours was a miracle.

Luckily, the show contains no sound cues, other than those provided onstage by actors. In the interest of minimizing the differences in audience experience between deaf and hearing, Diane elects, late in the game, to remove the few sound cues she had initially scripted. The most prominent of these is a police siren meant to accompany the revolving police light that closes Act One. Sounds can be translated by interpreters, but not, Diane feels, with any accuracy; better to leave them off entirely. The only two non-human sounds remaining are Krupke's police whistle and Chino's gun, a sound sufficiently concussive to be felt even by many of the profoundly deaf.

Mac's theater does not come supplied with loads of props. Even the retractable knives for "The Rumble" have to be ordered specifically for the show. Old china and cloth scraps are easy to find, but a blank firing pistol, one that will make "a good loud bang" without actually firing a bullet, proves to be something of a challenge. No one on the production team knows the first thing about guns, or where to get them. John Austin, the director of Theatre-works at IC, eventually agrees to loan Diane a .38-caliber firing pistol, but warns her that it "goes off like a cannon." Two test firings confirm John's impression, the second of which, conducted indoors, nearly costs this author his hearing. In the end, the crew locates a very serviceable .22-caliber revolver (again, a firing pistol) at a local military surplus shop. It doesn't have the dangerous punch of a bigger gun, but it does the job, and Tony, for the first time, actually looks—ironically, because of a sound—as if he's been shot.

Little improvements like these help bring Dane Vincent around, and his new, romantic involvement with Anna Poplett irons out any last remaining wrinkles. (Has any musical in the history of the United States ever been mounted without resulting in at least one backstage romance?) After the first weekend of performances, Dane is so pleased with both himself and the show in general that he e-mails Diane an unprompted apology letter that reads, in part:

> First off i would like to thank you for putting up with my anal retentive personality. . . . i just basically wanted to drop you a line to say thank you for letting me be in your show. Now you might think that this is a 360 degree turn from the beginning of the whole process (and it is) but it was true that i really didnt like the part chosen for me (but now i wouldn't trade it for the world) and i thought that a certain lady's directing skills lacked merit . . . but i was wrong so incredibly wrong. . . . i had heard all of these horror stories about how once people work with/for you they blatantly refuse to do so ever again. i partially wrote this to tell you that i am forever indebted to you and macmurray college for the opportunities given. in saying such i would like to extend my talents however meager they may be to you if you ever need them again all you have to do is ask. . . .
>
> Respectfully yours,
> Dante A. Vincent

Interpreting "Officer Krupke" proves to be a serious challenge. It is an exuberant, lively song, and the actors do not, should not, cannot stay still. Their constant mobility and bizarre overacting (street hoodlums pretending to be social workers, judges, policemen, etc.) creates havoc for the interpreters, who must follow as closely as they can without actually barging into the scene. Like "Tonight," this penalizes deaf audiences, who cannot easily watch both the interpreters and the crazed, manic expressions of the Jets. Even with Phil Fiorini's staging adjustments, expressly designed to assist deaf audiences, only the hearing audience members (able as they are to simultaneously watch and listen to the actors), are able to fully appreciate this fast-moving scene. The song's rampant use of idioms and double entendres is no help. Idioms in English often have no signable equivalent, and if they do, an interpreter might well have to fall back on what is sometimes referred to as "visual viewing," where said interpreter might sign the phrase "It's raining cats and dogs" by producing, in quick succession, the signs for rain, cats, and dogs. (To be sure, ASL also has its share of endemic idioms. One common one in the ISD classrooms is TRAIN GONE, or translated into English, "I already said that and you weren't listening, so that's your tough luck.") Phil works through the hash of jargon and double meanings as best he can, but partly because "Krupke" is a quick, fast-moving song, he allows the interpreters to rely on basic, generic signs for "*crazy*" far more often than either he or they would like. The result is that much of the song's verbal wit is lost on deaf viewers.

Still, the bulk of "Krupke" works for everyone, especially Christopher. The combination of highly theatrical movement combined with equally over-the-top zone signing (provided by the three *A*s, Andi, Allison, and Anna) fascinates him from the beginning. None of the Jets are trained dancers, but "Krupke" allows Christopher tremendous flexibility because the dancers do not need to sign as they dance—unlike "America" or "I Feel

Pretty." Instead, Christopher can develop what he calls the "physicality of the lyrical words," meaning that he has the freedom to lock in any sort of moves the Jet actors can handle. The relatively empty stage (four Jets, three interpreters), contributes to a wide-open approach, an approach quite different from crowded pieces like "The Prologue" or "Dance at the Gym," where the confines of the set dictate every move. Finally, because the Jets themselves rush around like dervishes, the interpreters suddenly have license to do the same, and it brings them to life in ways that much of the rest of the show fails to do. When the Jets yell out, "I'm disturbed!" the interpreters have the luxury of behaving at least as idiotically as the most lunatic Jet. As the song barrels to a finish (with the justly famous, "Gee, Officer Krupke—krup you!"), Jets and interpreters alike are reduced to a panting, ragged, kneeling line, and the audience—hearing and deaf alike—invariably responds with a burst of heartfelt applause. Unlike "Tonight," "Krupke" rises above its limitations and takes flight on something greater than the sum of its parts. As a triumph of ebullient acting and game coordination, it is a moment in which all communities can clearly be proud.

A Boy Like That!
I Have a Love

I remember Richard Rodgers' contribution. We had a death scene for Maria—she was going to commit suicide or something, as in Shakespeare. (Richard) said, "She's dead already, after this all happens to her."

Jerome Robbins[1]

Box office headaches plague *West Side Story* from the very minute that tickets go on sale. It has been more than two decades since any kind of Mac production has threatened to sell out, and no infrastructure exists to deal with the situation. Flora Bowe, an administrative assistant, gets the unlucky job of dispensing tickets. Diane takes the extraordinary step of creating a script for Flora to read to anyone seeking tickets. The text of the script reads:

> After taking their information, please inform the patron of the following:
>
> - The total amount billed to your credit card will be (Number of tickets _____ x $5): _____
>
> - These tickets are non-refundable and non-exchangeable.
>
> - You may pick up these tickets at the switchboard any time after February 15th, or you may pick them up at the door prior to the performance.

- The performance will be held in the Marian Chase Schaeffer Studio Theater on the first floor of the Education Complex.
- Seating is general (not assigned). While your ticket is guaranteed, we recommend that you arrive early to ensure the best possible seats.
- If you have questions about the production itself, please call the Studio Theater at 555-7208.

The script assumes that all callers will pay over the phone with credit cards, but Flora soon reports that many callers (some using a TTY, which Mac has had available for years) are leery of giving out credit card numbers and want to pay in person with cash or check. Diane agrees, but stresses that anyone reserving tickets without a credit card number must come in and pay for their tickets within twenty-four hours. After twenty-four hours, unpurchased tickets will go back into the general pool. Unfortunately, Flora does not always remember to inform potential buyers of the twenty-four-hour clause, so she begins holding tickets indefinitely. When the show officially sells out nine days before opening (with only ninety seats available in advance per night), Flora still has batches of tickets on hold for callers who have not replied in any way for over a month. Worse, Flora has no forwarding information—no phone numbers and no addresses. Diane fully expects that at least some of these people will show up, expecting to be seated, and it will then become her job—not Flora's—to turn them away at the door.

The doors themselves have been an issue since the inception of the steering committee. Early on, the production team makes a key concession to the physical limitations of the studio theater: actors will enter the stage area not merely from backstage, but from the outer doors of the room itself. The cast cannot fit into the narrow, cavelike backstage areas, and so a side hall, providing both an emergency exit for the theater and access to the building's electrical closet, becomes "a good place to store actors" and the de facto green room for the production run. This presents one somewhat alarming drawback in that the main door in and out of the theater will have to remain open not just for pre-show, post-show and intermission, but for the entire performance.

It's one thing to plot this in advance and quite another to grapple with the ramifications during dress rehearsals. For example, how will the ushers stop people from wandering in late? How can anyone anticipate the endless and unpredictable student activities just outside the confines of the theater? And, perhaps most pressing of all, how will the ushers and box office staff deal with the potential noise and arguments of any last-minute arrivals who insist—perhaps correctly so—that they were guaranteed tickets over the phone, and demand to be seated? Given the ongoing box office fiasco, it appears that some forty persons might well descend on the theater over the run of the show expecting to find tickets waiting in their name. Aside from placing these people first on the waiting list, there does not appear to be any sane strategy for dealing with this eventuality. Nor does there appear to be any way to silence—literally—any complaints they might make.

To help with the burgeoning nightmare of tickets, Diane gratefully accepts Heather Southwell's offer to handle the box office (really a rickety old table covered with a yellow paisley tablecloth, last seen by many as the centerpiece of Mrs. Alving's dining room in the fall production of *Ghosts*). Heather has joined Prentice on his Beardstown commute several times during rehearsals. A sociable woman with a ruddy, one-note laugh, Heather had volunteered to help early on, with the caveat that she wouldn't be able to actually contribute until late March. As a veteran of the Kansas City Blues Festival's box office, she seems perfect for the job. However, on Monday night, April 3, the night of the first dress rehearsal, a disturbing incident casts a pall over Heather—or anyone else—expected to watch over the cash box.

Jarrell Robinson and Prentice Southwell take a break during dress rehearsals.

Because of the limited size of the prop room and the lack of facilities and running water in the hallway-cum-green room, Diane has negotiated with the athletic department to secure locker room space on the first floor. The locker rooms will serve as the primary location for the actors to change, don their costumes and apply their makeup. Each actor receives a combination lock and Diane asks the cast members to stow all personal gear safely in their assigned lockers. The first trial of this somewhat involved system appears to have gone well until, with most of the cast already bound for home, Bryce reappears in the theater and informs Diane that his wallet is missing. Reluctantly, he admits to suspecting CJ. He doesn't like the thought, but CJ's locker is next to his, and CJ had been right there for the brief moment that Bryce removed his wallet and set it on the bench on top of his clothes. When Bryce turned back around, the wallet was gone, and with it, his driver's license, his lone credit card, and twelve dollars in cash.

Petty theft within a tightly knit group is always a disaster, and never more so than in a theatrical troupe. The process of learning roles and mounting a story requires tremendous trust; the development of that trust is a key part of any successful performance. Add one bad apple, or even the suspicion of such, and the whole enterprise can quickly unravel. Bryce understands full well what he has said and the ripple effect it will cause. He seems more torn about bringing it up than about the actual loss of his wallet. "He and I talk all the time," he says, referring to CJ, and he frowns at the floor, as if willing the entire situation to go quietly away. "I can't believe he'd do that to me."

Jen Harris, who has been folding costumes nearby, asks Diane if she has ever been made aware that CJ is officially required to be under special supervision. "He's supposed to have someone with him at all times," she explains, then adds, without clarification, that "he has a history of making bad decisions." Diane avows that she has never heard any such thing and that she certainly will call Steve Tavender the next morning to find out how to proceed. Jen suggests calling ISD immediately and having an on-duty dorm parent question CJ before morning. "If he took it, it'll be gone by tomorrow," she says.

Diane is exhausted and uncertain what else to do, so she picks up the theater telephone and makes the call. After replacing the receiver, she shakes her head. "I hope he didn't do it," she says. "Some people would get really offended if they got questioned about something like this. I think CJ will just roll with it. I hope he rolls with it."

Charles Johnson, who much prefers the shorter appellation of CJ, rolls with most things, sometimes in ways that do not please his mentors at ISD. He is eighteen but still a sophomore; repeating a year has become almost routine. His deafness is not severe, and he augments what hearing he has with speechreading. He dreams of playing professional hockey and expects to spend some upcoming free time at a hockey camp run by former

Olympic players, improving his skills and slamming pucks at any goalkeeper foolish enough to get in his way. He lacks a hockey player's bulk, but he is tall and, especially onstage, he is able to move with silken, dangerously suave movements that suggest he might well be a snake on ice. His narrow eyes rarely open fully. When they do, he sometimes looks a trifle startled.

In keeping with his other self-professed dream—becoming an actor—he cultivates a trim, narrow beard that runs in an exaggerated L down from his ears, across his jawline, and over to his chin. CJ doesn't look much like Gielgud or Olivier, but something about his beard and the smoothness of his skin suggests that he might suddenly assume the role of Hamlet and embark on a soliloquy over Yorick's lonely skull—a fitting image, given that CJ claims Shakespeare as his favorite writer. On Christopher Smith's suggestion, he hopes to spend the summer of 2001 eschewing hockey for an acting school in California run by Deaf West Theatre. If he attends, it will give him a chance to hone his decidedly underutilized skills. Before jumping into *West Side Story*, the last time CJ trod the boards was at the age of ten, and the part he played was that of a stationary tree.

When confronted by Chuck Nash about Bryce's wallet, CJ keeps his cool by rote. Maintaining a detached poise, as in *West Side Story*'s war council, his favorite scene, is a daily and carefully rehearsed aspect of his personality and life. He denies knowing anything about a missing wallet and counters Chuck's questions with an offer to help look for it. Chuck asks if CJ might know where to look, and CJ shrugs. "How would I know?" he says. "I'm not a thief, I didn't take it."

By the time the news reaches Steve Tavender, the harried wheels of justice have gone well past where he would like them to go. CJ has been through two interrogations already, and Steve can't help feeling that the entire episode is somehow off-kilter. Looking back, Steve remembers thinking, "'I guess it's possible,' but it just didn't make any sense. He had to have known it was too obvious, that everyone would look to him."

By the end of the day, the action that could have happened at the end of the previous night's rehearsal has been taken. Diane and Bryce, armed with a master list of combinations, search the lockers on either side of Bryce's. The wallet is not in CJ's locker. Instead, it turns up in the locker on the other side of Bryce's, belonging to Prentice Southwell. Nobody knows what to say, and Diane, Bryce, and ISD write off the entire matter as unintentional, because the wallet is trapped—but not enclosed or hidden—in the folds of Prentice's clothes. Diane tells Chuck and Steve to call off the dogs, but knows in her heart that it's already too late to fully salvage the situation. She feels bad, Steve and Chuck feel bad, and CJ deflates noticeably. His subsequent rehearsal performance suffers accordingly, and CJ-as-Bernardo carries all the threat of a limp balloon. The next night, however, he rebounds. "I want to keep the group as a family," he says, referring to the cast at large. "I know I'm not a thief. That's the end of it."

The set is nominally complete but looks naked. Most of the plywood and OSB board that went up in the third week of rehearsal has not been altered at all. The delay is due to a lack of snipes, *snipes* being the term advertisers (and disgruntled contractors) use to describe the cheaply printed advertising bills that get plastered all over construction zones in large cities. Snipes have been a key part of the set design from the beginning, and their messy but repetitive slogans are intended to decorate about half the set. The problem has been obtaining or even locating real snipes. Sniping is often put up quickly, with a squeegee and a bucket of glue. Once the posters adhere to a given surface, they can't be removed except by covering them over or ripping down the wall onto which they've been slapped. Ken Roumpos and Meredith Blair manage to abscond with a few during a spring break trip to New York City, but it isn't anywhere near enough.

The solution is Chicago printmaker Dan S. Wang, an artist with his own cylinder proof press. He agrees to create a series of five different fake snipes, and they arrive in short order. One describes an upcoming boxing match, another a featured DJ at a "local" club. At least two are tongue-in-cheek, the first reading "100% Effective, Call for Details" followed by a phone number, and the second reading "Vote Arroyo! Keep the West Side Clean!"

The sniping, combined with several imperative road signs (real ones, including "Stop" and "Do Not Enter"), turns the set from a pile of disconnected lumber into a unified street scene, gritty and expressionistically urban, but it has the added and unintentional effect of patterning the entire space. The foreground area around Doc's shop is especially problematic because the interpreters regularly line up against the now-sniped wall to perform their scenes. Because no one warned Dan S. Wang to do otherwise, the snipes have all been printed on light-colored paper, then inked in high-contrast black, brown, or green; against this sharp background, the interpreter's hands, even lit, are not always as visible as they ought to be. Given the choice of removing or retaining the snipes, Diane elects to keep them. Much of the action, she reasons, will be clear even without interpretation. Post-show audience surveys support her optimism, and no one singles out the snipes as a problem.

One unanticipated addition to the set comes after the first full-dress rehearsal, during which the backstage noise level is simply unacceptable and could easily be measured in whole decibels. The deaf actors—and more than a few of their hearing counterparts—simply have no concept of how to move quietly. Clad in dance shoes with hard soles, the cast clicks and scuffs its way from place to place; several cast members even practice their dance steps while standing mere yards away—albeit out of sight—from the front rows. With the budget perilously close to spiraling out of control, Diane decides to pirate every blanket and carpet scrap from home and tape them into a series of back-stage runways. To a surprising degree, the carpeting dampens the actors' footfalls. Backstage movement remains a problem throughout the production, particularly near the main doors and under the lowest of the scaffolds (where even the most petite actors have to crawl to get past), but now, for the first time, backstage silence, not noise, is the norm for the hearing as well as for the deaf.

Other noises, however, abound. The scaffolds, especially Maria's, squeak like demented metal mice. Getting in and out of the whitewashed bridal shop proves to be an enormous challenge for the Shark girls, one of whom, in random rotation, always seems to hit her head on either the interior light or on some part of the scaffold's bracing. Worst of all, ambient sounds from the rest of the building continue to filter in with alarming ease. Predicting these noises—a nonissue to half the cast and at least a third of the overall audience—is virtually impossible. The balcony immediately outside of the Marian Chase Schaeffer Studio Theater looks over a lobby that divides the basketball courts and the main swimming pool. Down a short hallway are the locker room labyrinths, and directly under the theater lies the school's smallish but well-equipped weight room. Suspending any and all athletic events during performances is out of the question, and the most that can be done is to silence the powerful stereo in the weight room. After that, the production is at the mercy of whatever else has been scheduled in the building.

On balance, *West Side Story* gets lucky. With thick black Duvateen curtains hung over the doors, very little outside noise drifts in, although the backlash from the diving boards sometimes fights its way up through the floor. The worst noise comes midshow during an actual performance when a screaming crew of students visiting from the Illinois School for the Visually Impaired (ISVI, also located in Jacksonville) troop through the lobby area. On another night, a surprise swimming-pool birthday party for a gaggle of eight-year-old girls threatens to be truly disastrous, but with some well-timed coaxing, the girls and their parents are ushered out of the lobby and into the pool where their thin, high voices fade to blessed inaudibility.

The irony of expending such energy on "hearing problems" is not lost on anyone in the production team. More than one person points out that there would be no problem at all with doing every show, every year, with the main doors flung wide, provided the entire cast and audience were deaf. It would, as one wag points out, make for a safer environment (easy escape in event of a fire) and it would keep the air moving.

Air is not a topic for which Diane has any reserves of humor. The education complex has had dysfunctional heating and air conditioning for as long as anyone can remember, and virtually every semester since Diane's arrival, she has been told—indeed, promised—that the vents and thermostats in the theater space will be fixed "before the next show." This has yet to happen, and the prospect of running upward of sixty lighting instruments (easily an all-time high, at least during her tenure) and then cramming one hundred spectators and thirty actors into such a small space is enough to give her nightmares. (Diane has good reason to believe that her production of *Ghosts* would have been a much greater success if both cast and audience had not been taxed to the limit by an appalling late-fall heat wave that turned performances into stifling endurance tests of sweat and discomfort.) Now, a new company has appeared on the scene with promises of a completely computerized system and a year-round in-theater temperature of seventy-two degrees. Starting two weeks before dress rehearsals, the vents come alive, and cool air literally shoots in. The interminable process of lighting the show suddenly becomes almost pleasant.

Lighting, however, is never without its problems. Despite a host of new lighting instruments, the lighting crew soon discovers that it doesn't have enough to adequately do the job. Most of the lighting instruments are reserved for creating a wash (an evenly lit flood of light intended to illuminate the bulk of the stage). *West Side Story* demands at least two basic washes, one for daylight scenes and the other for night, each with different gels across the face of the lighting instruments. A variety of blue gels stand in for night, and "bastard amber" and "straw" (among others) intermingle with blue to imitate daylight. In addition to instruments dedicated to the wash, "specials" are required to highlight individual actors or locations, prime examples being a bright white light to pick out Ken and Pearlene meeting at the dance, or the green-gelled spotlight aimed at the disco ball just before the "Dance at the Gym."

In the Mac/ISD production, the main wash is more than sufficient to light the stage, but most of the play is supposed to take place at night, and with the resultant lower light levels, dark patches threaten to completely swallow interpreted lines and leave voicers in a morass of shadows. More specifically, two moments simply demand more light—and lighting instruments—than the facility can provide. The first of these instances takes place as Tony kisses Maria good night in their modernized, fire escape equivalent of *Romeo and Juliet*'s balcony scene. Just before Tony leaves, Maria teaches him the sign for *"I love you,"* and they press their fingers together in a matching, mirrored tableau. Unfortunately, the scaffold is set at the back of the stage, and even in the confines of such a small theater, Diane worries that the gesture will never be seen. This is particularly upsetting because, for her, this is the single most important moment in the play—the instant where Tony begins to learn ASL. The crew attempts to rig another spotlight, but soon discovers there is no independent channel remaining on the light board, which renders the additional unit useless.

A nearly identical problem crops up in the second act, when Anita and Maria sign and sing their linked songs, "A Boy Like That" and "I Have a Love." The scene is sufficiently bright, but the boundaries of the lit area are too small, and both Olivia (as Anita) and Pearlene (as Maria) continually swing their hands and arms outside the beam of light. Because the background is black, any movements made outside the light are lost from view. The crew gives the two actors a center mark to hit, but Pearlene, who depends on visual cues from Andi to pace herself, complains that when she stands on her marks, the light blinds her and she can't see Andi. Diane and Phil compensate by asking Pearlene to keep her movements closer to her torso, but it simply isn't enough. If more lighting instruments were available, added they would be, but every bulb in the theater is now in use (including two "practicals," household lamps normally used by the crew to light basic projects like cutting wood and building theatrical flats). Diane grits her teeth in frustration; even the lights—the purview of sight, not sound—dare to undermine her work.

After some deliberation, the production team concludes that the only way to address the lighting issues in a meaningful way would be to acquire a new lighting board, one with more available control channels, and maybe renting extra lighting instruments. With the budget already stretched to the proverbial limits, neither option is actually feasible, and so the show soldiers on as is, poorly lit warts and all.

A flurry of last-minute sound-related issues crop up, each one tumbling quickly on top of the next. Terri rents an electric keyboard to replace the old clunker of an upright that has been her darling for the past three months. After a quick tour of the keys, Terri determines that the keyboard, which had sounded good enough as an in-store display, is simply not up to the task. She consults with Jay Peterson, and Jay obtains a well-tuned, well-maintained upright from the rehearsal rooms on the far side of campus. Jay then drops a minor but last-minute bombshell on Terri by asking her to use the services of several current music majors as page turners during the show. Terri had planned to rely on her daughters, Rachel, 15, and Laura, 12, both of whom read music and know the score well, having attended numerous rehearsals in the preceding months. (Rachel and Laura wanted to attend even more often than they did, and had it not been for homework, Terri would have gladly accepted their assistance every night.) In the end, Terri decides to honor Jay's request, which means that she will have to work with three new page turners, none of whom know the score. This, of course, is precisely why Jay wants his students to take on the job—to pick their way through a musical cold reading. Terri sees other dangers, namely, that her new page turners will be so fascinated by the action onstage that they won't pay close enough attention to the work at hand. Her fears prove to be well-founded but not disastrous; she gets through the remaining rehearsals with a series of carefully timed nudges and little breathy hisses that, if translated into English, would clearly mean, "Turn that page! Now!"

Finale

I've always believed that the climax of a musical should be musicalized. Well, the climax of *West Side Story* is not musicalized. It's a speech I wrote as a dummy lyric for an aria for Maria, with flossy words about guns and bullets. It was supposed to be set to music, and it never was.

Arthur Laurents[1]

Monday, April 3 and Tuesday, April 4

The second dress rehearsal. The majority of the cast is not pleased with the run-through, but Diane, concerned with morale and the wear and tear on the singer's voices, announces at the end of Monday night that the next night's rehearsal will be canceled. "Take the night off," she says. "Relax."

Dane Vincent, who has already left for his night shift at the Amerihost, never gets the message, and no one thinks to call him the next day. He shows up on schedule and wonders why Carrie hasn't arrived to open the doors. Eventually he gets the idea that no one else is coming and heads for the dining hall, where Charlie Smerz works in the kitchen. Charlie informs him that a group of students plans to watch the film of *West Side Story* later that night, and invites Dane to join them. The movie is a hit, and the little group breaks into song more than once. By the end, Dane has an epiphany: not only can he play Diesel and Big Deal, but he can also play the role of Ice. Ice, who sings "Cool" in the film and takes over the Jets after Riff's death, does not exist in the libretto for the play. He is, however, everything that Dane has wanted his part to be: powerful, unflappable, a leader. Without overtly altering his character, Dane internalizes Ice—the philosophy of "Cool" personified—and discovers, for the first time in weeks, a sense of contentment.

Wednesday, April 5

A semi-invited preview audience, consisting of Charlie Smerz's friends from Jacksonville High, files in and takes seats, not knowing what to expect. Diane warns them at the outset, "This is still a rehearsal. I may even stop the play, give directions. But I think I won't have to." Aside from a few quick comments during scene changes, her optimism proves to be well-founded. The show runs smoothly, but at the end, during the curtain call, it is clear that the actors long for a bigger response than Charlie's friends can provide. They hold out the hope that the next night, a sold-out preview showing for ISD's junior and high schools, will provide some public recognition.

Thursday, April 6

Unofficially opening night, and the house is dominated by ISD's junior high students. The play begins, as Diane has planned nearly from the start, with silence. The lights fade to black and Baby John, with a basketball, climbs the most distant painter's scaffold. Once he's seated, a single spotlight picks him out of the background, but he doesn't move. He doesn't speak. He doesn't whistle. Instead, he simply considers the ball in his hands—and he takes his time. Then, as if fed up with both the ball and life itself, he flings the basketball out into the darkness.

At the moment that the ball hits the floor, a wash of lights rises to reveal Riff as he steps out from behind a wall of sniping. He and

Diesel and Riff (Charlie Smerz) parley with Chino and Bernardo (Christopher Smith and Charles Johnson).

Baby John exchange a coded greeting, wordless, a sign language specific only to themselves, and one by one the other Jets arrive for a quick, impromptu basketball game—a game played out, from start to finish, in silence. When Terri's piano finally kicks in with a series of abrupt triplets, the Jets take to snapping their fingers, keeping the beat for the Sharks as the rival gang struts onto the stage. Richard Fee hovers in the wings, ready to burst on as Schrank and stop the ensuing fight. While he waits, he begins his nightly countdown of shows. Seven to go, he tells himself; only seven more chances to make a mistake and blow it all. Only seven more chances to holler and yell.

Later, at the end of the first act, Christopher (as Chino) flees up and over the lower scaffold, just as he always does when the police lights come into view. This time, however, he skids, trips, and hurtles over the far edge, landing directly on top of Meredith, who is about to dash on as Anybodys and drag Tony away from Riff's body. Meredith sports a pair of ugly bruises on her upper arm for the rest of the run, but Christopher, who was moving fast and fell several feet onto the solid two-by-tens that make up the stairs, escapes without a scratch.

The audience response is enthusiastic, but not remarkably so. The students in attendance are generally younger than those on the stage, and most of the ISD actors' close friends and peers will not see the show until April 12. Many people fill out response cards in the lobby after the show, but nothing on the slips of paper asks the reviewers to identify themselves by name, age, or level of hearing. Most of those who turn in cards do so anonymously, making the collected opinions (mostly positive) impossible to track. The real test, as everyone seems to understand, will be the next night, with a full house of a mixed hearing and deaf audience—exactly the audience that the production team has taken aim at all along.

Friday, April 7

Opening night. No one, not even Richard Atkins's parents, gets in off the waiting list. Diane reluctantly turns them away at the door as a greater-than-capacity crowd swells into unplanned seats that almost certainly, to a savvy observer, allow for sight line problems and glimpses of backstage activity. Diane fills what chairs she can, saying, "I'd rather have them see the show than complain that they couldn't get in."

The show begins. The show runs. The show ends. The awful moment between blackout and applause lingers, refusing to go away. Perhaps no director or creative team ever fully knows whether they have a hit until the final curtain. In this moment, more than any other, the Mac production team stands beside Bernstein, Robbins, Laurents, and Sondheim. It's forty-three years later, but the questions are the same. Will it sink or will it swim? The work is complete, the story finished; all that remains is the hope for affirmation.

The lights come up and the curtain call begins. The audience responds immediately, delivering not merely applause, but a standing ovation. Deaf audience members clap for hearing performers, then when applauding deaf actors, they wave their hands in the air and keep their fingers outstretched. More than a few hearing audience members imitate the gesture, or already know to vary their response according to the hearing level of the actors. The enthusiasm, the pride and goodwill, are palpable, they hang in the air like a benediction. By the time the applause dies down, Diane is near tears—as is a large segment of the audience. "Wonderful," says one woman, dabbing at her cheeks as she makes her way outside. "I don't know why I can't stop crying."

One definitive reason for the tears is Pearlene, who pulls out all the stops as she crouches over Tony's body. She signs her grief so fiercely that the gang members looking on have to jump out of her way, and her voice, never used at any other point in the show, comes alive in a keening shriek. The sounds that fly from her throat rip through the room like a saw cutting metal, and for those who can hear it, it is genuinely terrifying, a tremendous finish to a challenging show. The production team's consensus: Pearlene has learned to act. And how.

Saturday, April 8

Another standing ovation. Good show, overall, except that Charlie has left his actor's spurs back at the proverbial greenhorn's ranch. He drops a line early on, then minces both the lyrics and his vocal technique while singing in "Quintet/Tonight." Carrie passes a note to Diane (because no audience seats remain, Diane has joined Carrie and Nathan in the control booth). The note reads, "What's wrong with Charlie tonight?" Diane's response: "Don't know. At least he dies soon."

Not, however, soon enough. As sometimes happens with inexperienced actors, one mistake simply leads to another in an ever-evolving spiral of worry and self-doubt. Sure enough, Charlie forgets to bring out his knife for "The Rumble." Terri notices first. Pulling the knife is a major cue for her, a switch into a new, dramatic chord, and she can see quite plainly that Charlie's waistband is empty. When CJ flashes his knife, Charlie just spreads his hands, as if to say, "Whoops. Looks like you've got a weapon and I don't." Terri begins regardless, and Charlie and CJ improvise their way through the stabbing, heavily abbreviating the resultant action. Everyone dies on schedule, but Christopher's well-rehearsed choreography goes out the window.

During intermission, a backstage controversy erupts over how to conduct the dream sequence of "Somewhere," where the gangs reenact the rumble. Should the combatants come out with one knife or two? In the end, they go with one, leaving Michael Nesmith (who plays the dream version of Tony in the ballet sequence) with the difficult task of killing CJ by breaking his neck. They rehearse throughout intermission and the results work well enough onstage. When Diane corners Charlie after the show and offers a fresh round of suggestions for how he can hold his focus, Charlie, for the first time ever, gives her his full attention.

Phil picks this run to begin his nightly attempts to tease Andi into breaking character. Whenever Andi is onstage, Phil hovers in the wings, just out of the audience's view but very much in Andi's line of sight. Once there, he makes faces, sticks out his tongue, and signs various lewd and repulsive comments. In scenes where Phil and Andi work together, Phil finds ways of making equally ridiculous expressions just before the lights come up or the dialogue begins. Andi holds her own, but friends in the audience who know her best realize something is up. After the show, one asks, "How come you were smirking all the time?" Andi rolls her eyes and introduces Phil, who has, racy interruptions aside, become a trusted friend. From Phil, she's learned where to look as an onstage interpreter, how to be active but not distracting, how to present herself. Her tendency to look not at the action onstage, but at the ground, might never have been caught and quashed without Phil's intervention. The process has been a revelation, a vocabulary builder, a lesson in pedagogy, and culture shock—all in all, exactly what she wants out of her future interpreting career. It is a career that already threatens to lead her back to theater; at Diane's behest, Phil and Andi already have plans to reunite for Mac's fall production of *Antigone*. This gives Andi six months to devise and exact on Phil a suitably Sophoclean revenge.

The next morning, at Centenary Methodist Church, a friend approaches Terri Benz, and before Terri can say so much as, "Good morning," the friend exclaims, "I have not stopped thinking about *West Side Story* all night. Now I understand why you couldn't describe it!"

Sunday, April 9

The one and only matinee. Daylight leaks in around the doors, also through the grille of a return duct from the cooling system. The lobby area around the natatorium is appallingly loud. Somehow, everyone summons the energy to overcome the new schedule. Dane, who never made it to bed since leaving work, stumbles through the performance, but avoids accidentally singing, as he did one night during rehearsals when the lines of "Officer Krupke" escaped him, about his sister's gross anatomy.

Hollie Lovell, the student in charge of props, turns away a woman who shows up just after the house has closed. Diane has assigned a house manager for every show to guard against late entrants or other disturbances, and at this performance, Hollie has drawn the shortest straw. The woman, who has two small children with her, one barely a toddler, is not the first to show up late and be denied both her ticket and a seat, but she is the first to become angry. Her complaints can easily be heard by those sitting nearest the door—at least, by those with hearing—and she refuses, for some time, to take no for an answer. Hollie, who looks as sweet as apple pie, doesn't give an inch, and eventually the woman retreats, towing her five-year-old daughter along by her wrist. Her parting shot: "My daughter is deaf and she has a right to see this show!"

Wednesday, April 12

The most remarkable show of all. ISD's deaf high schoolers and a number of ISD faculty and dorm parents comprise virtually the entire audience. The Sharks respond with by far their best—and raunchiest—performance. All the original lines remain intact, but tonight they are peppered with secret signs, epithets, sexual innuendo, and flagrant swearing sign-style. The in-the-know audience can't believe they're seeing their own local cant, in all its crude and blatant glory, displayed in public. By the time the show is over, the audience has taken to actively booing the Jets and cheering the Sharks. Richard Fee maintains that this was the night the ISD actors finally came alive, that this was the first time they became full partners and found themselves on equal footing with their hearing compatriots. In general, he feels that the Sharks were handcuffed by the script, in particular in Schrank's presence, since their chief response in the face of adult authority is nonresponse. Finally, with a deaf audience capable of interpreting their every gesture, the deaf actors could respond. And respond they did. More than one adult audience member—aware of the local dialects through contact with or proximity to ISD—leaves the theater both moved and appalled. "I can't believe they did that," one (hearing) woman says. She does not specify a scene or a sign, but she leaves us with the power of imagination: "That was *disgusting*!"

Paula Chance corners Christopher after the show and peppers him with questions, compliments, and a few wistful complaints. She loves the set—"Nice props!"—but wishes the music had been louder, preferably amplified. Why didn't Diane use drums? She wanted to feel the beat in the same way that she felt the soundtrack from the movie, a score that she describes as "more rock and roll," but then shrugs whimsically and says, "Of course, I don't have any idea of what that really means."

Because she couldn't feel the music, she found the singing boring, it "slowed everything down." She kept wanting to interrupt and stamp her foot to demand that the singers hurry up and get on with it. But at least her worries about gangs turned out to be unfounded. "Why wasn't I more open-minded?" she asks, then half answers herself with, "I pride myself on being open-minded." Oh, and the interpreters, they were too fast, too hurried! Diane should have stuck to using professionals, "like Kreps and that Paul guy. No, not Paul. Phil. Kreps and Phil, they were great."

Of the ISD students, Paula was most impressed with Jeanne Kujawa—"In school, she's so quiet!"—and CJ, whom she describes as a chronically sloppy signer, but not, it appears, on the stage. Olivia, she feels, was not so clear. Did she even understand what she was saying? All that signed English!

For Christopher Smith, Paula has nothing but admiration. Good job, she tells him. When do we do it again?

Thursday, April 13

Before the show begins, Diane, walking amongst the actors as they prep their makeup, notices a funny smell, a smell that emanates from Dane Vincent. Dane, it turns out, has never once given up his costume to be washed, and now it stinks, reeking of sweat. Other actors give him a wide berth, make cracks, and hold their noses. Diane responds by handing Dane a spray bottle of Febreze. "Put this on," she orders. "Right now!"

Prominent community members are out in force. Jacksonville's chief of police attends, also Mac president Larry Bryan and ISD's Steve Tavender. Larry Bryan later sends a note, as he always does, telling Diane that he enjoyed the performance. No elaboration, no specifics. He never stays after the curtain call to make comments or say hello. Steve, however, is effusive. "I never knew you were so talented!" he gushes, and then hurries off to greet each of "his" students. For her part, Diane lets the compliment go. Despite the show's evident success—the great pleasure it gives to its audience—she wonders if she really did anything more than "direct traffic." When another person tries to praise her work, she shakes her head, lets her hair fly around her face, and stares sideways at the floor. She insists that the performers should get the credit. And she reminds the cast, as she has every night, that they mustn't in any way recognize her during the curtain call. The first time she told them this, the cast took offense, thinking she wasn't proud of them, or the show. Diane begs them to understand that this is not the case. "It's simply not how it's done in professional theater," she tells them, "and it would make me very uncomfortable."

Friday, April 14

The worst the show has been since early dress rehearsals. Summer is stepping on spring's toes, and suddenly the air conditioning is unresponsive; it later proves to be off entirely. A little detective work soon reveals that the company that had so recently and successfully installed the new, computerized air conditioning system has just been bought out by a corporation based in Texas—a corporation that has no further plans to service the education complex. The heat builds and builds until the actors onstage are dripping—Ken and Dane, in particular, are drenched—and audience members, especially in the upper rows, resort to fanning themselves with their programs. Attention wanders, concentration lags. To cap the evening, Christopher (as Chino) rushes onstage to shoot Tony, and the gun won't go off.

He tries twice, glances suspiciously at the barrel, and attempts to fire a final time. Ken gets the message, pretends he's heard the shots, and collapses on cue. Later, more than one member of the audience confesses that they thought this was entirely intentional. Given a show with no prerecorded sound cues, a silent gun seems eminently logical.

At least one audience member is unaffected by the heat. A hearing six-year-old boy, sitting just in front of the control booth, watches the opening of the ballet and suddenly realizes that the actors are about to reenact "The Rumble," and that the results, danced or not, will be just as tragic as before. With undisguised worry in his voice, he says, to no one in particular, "Oh, no. They're doing it again." Next to him, his mother begins to cry.

Friday's show proves to be the only night that does not garner a standing ovation. Diane, emerging from her cramped seat in the control booth, looks positively ill. Not everyone feels so unhappy. Pearlene's mother stands in the hallway, elated, and signs to anyone who will look at her, "I can't believe my daughter is *singing*!"

Saturday, April 15

Closing night. Hours before the show begins, Diane drags a gigantic fan up from the athletic department and stations it in the theater's back doorway. With the fan running full blast, the room cools, but not quickly. It's a warm day, eighty degrees, and the roof of the theater continues to heat like a baking stone until just before sunset. Nathan and Carrie run through the pre-show light check with the master set at 30 percent. The actors conduct their warm-ups in the hall, and the house does not open until a mere ten minutes before curtain—anything to keep the room from heating up any sooner than it has to. All the precautions help, but not much; the air conditioning remains dormant, and the temperature rises steadily throughout the first act. This time, however, perhaps because the actors know in advance what to expect, they persevere and refuse to droop. The evening ends with one last standing ovation, a bouquet of flowers for Terri Benz, and an incisive, two-hour strike that leaves the room looking as if it were trying, once again, to become a quiet little fencing gym.

Two weeks later, the cast and crew reassemble for a lazy, almost sedate barbecue-cum-cast-party on the Mac lawn. It's eighty-five degrees and humid; weather maps show potent rainstorms in all directions. CJ tries to catch Frisbees in his teeth; Michael brings a skateboard and then doesn't use it. Olivia chases a soccer ball, only to be chased in turn by Cara Hammond's lively little sheltie. Bob Dramin and his wife bring their children; everyone coos over his youngest. Diane spots an enormous ring glittering on Pearlene's left hand, a ring featuring the traditional masks of tragedy and comedy.

"Pearlene," Diane asks, amazed, "are you married?"

Ever the coquette, Pearlene proudly replies, "I'm married to drama!"

Pearlene's enjoyment is marred, however, by the fact that Ken, who is deeply engaged in a discussion with Melanie Jacobson over the subject of choir politics, never makes an effort to chat. She thinks to herself that it's just like in the movies, where the two actors, so in love on screen, must go their separate ways once the filming is complete. Stung, she talks to everyone else she can find, including Bryce Hoffman, who tells her that he has decided, as a result of *West Side Story*, to become a Deaf Ed major.

This is the last official function of the West Side Storiers, but, for many, the reunion is muted by the unexpected death that morning of Phil Decker. Phil, Diane's theatrical progenitor and perhaps the most popular professor Mac has ever known, had been quietly fighting lung cancer since November 1999. He was the first person at MacMurray to hear the fledgling idea of staging *West Side Story* as a "deaf" musical, and the first to offer his encouragement. In the end, his illness prevented him from seeing so much as a single rehearsal.

Later, Diane takes leave of the cast party early in order to attend the first of her expectant parent classes at Springfield's Memorial Hospital. As she speeds toward the city, racing between field after field of barely sprouted bright green corn, she remembers exactly what Phil Decker told her, all those months ago, upon hearing that only half of *West Side Story*'s cast would themselves be hearing.

"That's a great idea," he said. "Go do it."

Epilogue

November 2002

The production is long gone. At least half of Mac's student body has no memory of *West Side Story* having ever happened and, what with the cast and crew having scattered to the four winds, much the same situation applies at ISD. Such is the nature of theater.

No one understands this better than Christopher, who has returned to Gallaudet to continue taking classes and center himself in the bower of the area's large and welcoming Deaf community. He has never stopped performing, and his induction into the Wild Zappers, an all-deaf, all-male dance troupe, recently took him to Los Angeles to perform for that city's Deaf Expo. The Wild Zappers work most often along the Atlantic seaboard, but they have traveled to Australia, Jamaica, and Japan, among others, and they have appeared in venues across the United States, winning numerous awards and garnering an appearance on *The New Kaptain Kangaroo*. Each member of the Zappers, formed in 1989, contributes to the choreography, and while in Los Angeles, two of Christopher's pieces were featured, "Out Here on My Own," (the theme from *Fame*) and "Strange Fruit," as sung by Billie Holiday. When he's not on tour, Christopher works as an office assistant for Invisible Hands, the brainchild of Fred Michael Beam, cofounder of the Wild Zappers. Invisible Hands, an ambitious nonprofit group, is "dedicated to the advancement of deaf and cultural awareness and to bridging the gap between the hearing and deaf communities"—a perfect fit for Christopher.

Christopher's early skittishness in speaking about his past
(or even his present) has undergone a seismic shift of late, for he
is about to star in *This*, a new play written by Raymond Luczak—
and "this" means Christopher, as the play is based on his own life
history. As Christopher writes, "Raymond Luczak, he is also deaf
himself too, very good friend of mine. It is somewhat based on
true story of me and my late best friend, that we were struggling
being deaf, black . . . artist[s] in New York City. In those days, the
world wasn't ready for us or who we are. So, that's basically what's
the story is all about. It will be happening in January" 2003.
In the meantime, he continues to perform his one-man show,
Fingers of Broken Dreams, an autobiographical performance piece
told through dance and music.

Pearlene Jo Theriot, who now enjoys using her last name
when possible, has also continued her stage work, and *West Side
Story* has served as inspiration in creating her own original theater piece, *Tonight*:

> After my sophomore year at Illinois School for the Deaf, I relocat-
> ed to Model Secondary School for the Deaf (MSSD) for the last
> two years of high school. There, I co-directed and performed a
> different version of *West Side Story*. It was a different experience
> because we all were deaf and in high school. . . . *Tonight* was
> MSSD's annual spring play production directed and staffed by
> only students. Garret Bose, also a student, and I directed about
> 20 other students. The audience was the gallaudet university com-
> munity which included kendall school, mssd . . . alumnis, neigh-
> bors, family and friends from around the city . . . the play was
> 2 hours. . . . It was a big production that I decided to take a year off
> from performing afterwards and might be participating in the
> Gallaudet University's Spring Production.

Pearlene's self-professed hatred of music has mellowed, although
her focus on music remains, unsurprisingly, on the words. The
songs she memorized for *West Side Story* "play in my head
often up to today! Some of the lyrics apply to my daily
living situations once in a while and boosts my days!" Dance is

still something of a bugbear, although she feels she is "doing better."

Looking back at *West Side Story* leaves Pearlene wondering what the experience would have been like had she been older. She turned fifteen during rehearsals, and, as she puts it, "Fourteen years old are inclined to be most shy performing some smooch-smooch love scenes than when they are in COLLEGE!!!!!!!!!!!!!! Hence, I feel that if I perform now, it would be flashier! (Wink)." In a 2002 e-mail, she signs off with, "Always Maria, Pearlene Jo Theriot."

Mac and ISD have not mounted any further artistic collaborations. Steve Tavender is set to retire at the end of the fall 2002 academic semester, and Diane Brewer has already moved on, to the University of Evansville in Evansville, Indiana. Mac, despite a brand-new music and arts facility, continues to battle enrollment issues, and as a result, a number of faculty positions have been phased out, including that of the college chaplain—ironic, in that Mac remains a church-affiliated school. Terri Benz, who began teaching music at Mac shortly after *West Side Story* finished, now pulls double-duty as the college's part-time Director of Religious Life. Even though she was with the *West Side Story* production from beginning to end, her initial challenge of "I just want to see how you're going to pull this off!" still awaits an answer. She looks back today with the same wonderment as when she began, confessing she is "amazed that we were able to make it work!" Ever humble, Terri describes "a great well of respect for all the cast members, but mostly for those who couldn't hear Diane's direction [and] for those who acted with everything they had."

Diane's place on the Mac faculty has been taken by Nancy Taylor, who, like Diane when she first arrived, is fresh off her dissertation work (at Tufts University in Boston). Under Nancy's stewardship, Mac has produced Paula Vogel's Pulitzer Prize-winning *How I Learned to Drive* and classics like the Bard's *Measure for Measure*, among others. All of this information is easily retrieved from Mac's Web page, which as of December 2002, still contains a paragraph on the *West Side Story* project. The last line of the write-up states: "We're very excited about the results and hope to do something similar in the future."

Diane, busy with work and parenthood, has been back to Jacksonville and the Mac campus only once since moving away. She vacillates between being exceptionally pleased with her new department (nine people total, whereas at Mac she was a program of one) and aiming self-critical barbs at the relative safety of her choice. *West Side Story* pushed boundaries, challenging her, the production team, the cast and the community. Her next trip to the directorial plate will be with A. R. Gurney's *Sylvia*—a play that she enjoys, but she has no expectations that it will have a lasting impact on the community at large. Opportunities for riskier choices are limited. Evansville's program, for undergraduates only, is outstanding, and the caliber of work they produce has a polish and consistency that many drama programs would give their right arm to achieve, but Diane cannot help searching the horizon for a way to incorporate something just a little crazy into the department's solid, surefooted repertoire.

Would she ever remount *West Side Story*, again with a mixed deaf and hearing cast? No, not likely. But, she says with a smile, "Let's just say I know there is a Deaf community in Evansville."

We were teamed up beautifully. Especially it was very new experiences for both of us to brainstorm our ideas tirelessly. I sensed that we both had the same understanding regardless being deaf and hearing to bridge the gap. It has something to do with chemistry to work together itself.

Christopher Smith
November 2, 2002

I believe that a good director creates opportunities for collaboration
. . . and I believe we had some really good collaboration going on.

Diane Brewer
May 26, 2000

End Credits

CAST

Jets

Tony..Ken Roumpos
Riff..Charlie Smerz
Action..Richard Atkins
Diesel..Dane Vincent
A-Rab..Prentice Southwell
Baby John...Bryce Hoffman

Sharks

Bernardo ....Charles Johnson
Chino..Christopher Smith
Pepe..Patrick Baker
Louis...Michael Nesmith
Anxious..Jarrell Robinson

Shark Girls

Maria ....Pearlene Jo
Anita ....Olivia Frome
Rosalia ....Amy Dignan
Consuela ....Jeanne Kujawa
Francisca ....April Garvey

Jet Girls

Anybodys ....Meredith Blair
Velma..Jennifer Harris

Graziella ....Dawn Williams
Clarice ....Anna Poplett
Minnie ....Helen Brattain

The Adults
Doc ....Jay Peterson
Lt. Schrank...Richard Fee
Officer Krupke..Jeannie Zeck
Glad Hand ....April Garvey

Sign Language Interpreters
Tony ....Phil Fiorini
Riff, A-Rab, Doc, Schrank ....Andi Kreps
Diesel, Baby John, Graziella ....Allison Titus
Krupke, Action, Anybodys, Velma............................Anna Poplett

Voice Interpreters
Maria ....Dawn Williams
Anita...Meredith Blair
Rosalia ....Anna Poplett
Consuela ....Helen Brattain
Francisca..Jennifer Harris
Bernardo..Matt Fraas
Chino. ....Richard Atkins
Glad Hand..Andi Kreps
Pepe ....Bryce Hoffman

Production Team
Director...Diane Brewer
Choreographer..Christopher Smith
Music Director ....Terri Benz
Technical Director/Designer ....Mark Rigney
Vocal Consultant..Melanie Jacobson
Stage Managers ....Carrie Moore, Nathan Grieme
Co-Lighting Designer...Teresa McCarthy
Co-Set Designer..Meredith Blair
Costume Designers...........................Jennifer Harris, Meredith Blair

Props ....Hollie Lovell
Set Crew ....Teresa McCarthy, Laura Grawe
                                    Rob Shaffer, Jennifer Wellhausen
Lighting Crew ....Teresa McCarthy, Laura Grawe
                        Jamae Lindsay, Jennifer Wellhausen, K. Witt
Light Board Operator..Nathan Grieme
Makeup Design..Maria Gullo
Makeup Assistants ....Chandra McDonald, Joanna Bush
Rehearsal Interpreter ....Becky Cline
Program/Poster Design ....Milly Clinton
Contributing Set Artist..Dan S. Wang

Notes

Jet Song

1. Nanci A. Scheetz, *Orientation to Deafness* (Boston: Allyn & Bacon, 1993), 197.

2. Stanley Rosenberg, cited by the Associated Press. BBC News Online (Education) 11/29/99. Available: http://news.bbc.co.uk/1/hi/education/541882.stm

3. Robert Matthew-Walker, *From Broadway to Hollywood: The Musical and the Cinema* (London: Sanctuary, 1996), 212.

4. Meryle Secrest, *Leonard Bernstein: A Life* (New York: Alfred A. Knopf, 1994), 215.

5. Pauline Kael, *I Lost It at the Movies* (Boston: Little, Brown, 1965), 142-43.

6. Joan Peyser, *Bernstein: A Biography* (New York: Beech Tree, 1987), 13.

Something's Coming

1. Otis L. Guernsey, Jr., *Broadway Song and Story: Playwrights/Lyricists/Composers Discuss Their Hits* (New York: Dodd, Mead & Company, 1985), 45.

Dance at the Gym

1. Ronnie B. Wilbur, "The Use of ASL to Support the Development of English and Literacy," *Journal of Deaf Studies and Deaf Education* 5 (winter 2000): 82.

2. Scheetz, *Orientation to Deafness*, 200.

3. Ibid., 201.

4. Ibid., 47-148.

5. Ibid., 201.

6. Carol Musselman, "How Do Children Who Can't Hear Learn to Read an Alphabetic Script?" *Journal of Deaf Studies and Deaf Education* 5 (winter 2000): 25.

7. Ibid., 26.

8. Ibid.

Maria

1. Guernsey, *Broadway Song and Story*, 46.

America

1. Scheetz, *Orientation to Deafness*, 1.

2. Ibid., 111.

3. McCay Vernon and Jean F. Andrews *The Psychology of Deafness: Understanding Deaf and Hard-of-hearing People* (New York: Longman, 1990), 72.

4. Beryl Lieff Benderly, *Dancing Without Music* (Washington, D.C.: Gallaudet University Press, 1990), 1.

5. Douglas C. Baynton, *Forbidden Signs: American Culture and the Campaign against Sign Language* (Chicago: University of Chicago Press, 1996), 16.

6. Alexander Graham Bell, quoted in Baynton, *Forbidden Signs*, 136.

7. Baynton, *Forbidden Signs*, 135.

8. Ibid., 150-51.

9. Emma Garrett cited in Baynton, *Forbidden Signs*, 152.

Cool/Tonight

1. Don Michael Randel, *The Harvard Concise Dictionary of Music and Musicians* (Cambridge: Belknap Press of Harvard University Press, 1999), 296.

2. *Merriam-Webster's Collegiate Dictionary*, 10th ed., s.v. "hemiola."

One Hand, One Heart

1. Scheetz, *Orientation to Deafness*, 275.

Quintet (Tonight Medley)

1. Humphrey Burton, (quoting Brooks Atkinson), *Leonard Bernstein* (New York: Doubleday Books, 1994), 276.

2. *Webster's Encyclopedic Unabridged Dictionary of the English Language*, rev. ed., s.v. "cacophony."

The Rumble

1. Secrest, *Leonard Bernstein*, 217.

I Feel Pretty

1. Diane Brewer, "West Side Silence: Producing *West Side Story* with Deaf and Hearing Actors," *Theatre Topics* 12 (winter 2002).

Gee, Officer Krupke

1. Guernsey, *Broadway Song and Story*, 50.

A Boy Like That/I Have a Love

1. Guernsey, *Broadway Song and Story*, 43.

Finale

1. Guernsey, *Broadway Song and Story*, 44.

About the Author

Author photo by Gerard Brewer

Mark Rigney is the author of several plays, including the prize-winning *Lines in the Sand*, and his short fiction has appeared in venues such as *THEMA* and the *Bellevue Literary Review*. He has worked as a zookeeper, a film industry sound recordist, and a retail trainer; he is now proud to be a stay-at-home father.

CPSIA information can be obtained
at www.ICGtesting.com
Printed in the USA
FFOW03n1637071014
7871FF